BRAIN BOOSTER
MATHS

DK UK
Senior Editors Sarah MacLeod Bailey, Rebecca Fry
Senior Designers Phil Gamble, Jessica Tapolcai
Illustrator Phil Gamble
Managing Editor Carine Tracanelli
Managing Art Editor Anna Hall
Jackets Design Development Manager Sophia MTT
Production Editor Gill Reid
Senior Production Controller Poppy David
Art Director Karen Self
Publisher Andrew Macintyre
Publishing Director Jonathan Metcalf

DK INDIA
Jacket Designer Rhea Menon
DTP Designer Deepak Mittal
Senior Jackets Coordinator Priyanka Sharma Saddi

First published in Great Britain in 2024 by
Dorling Kindersley Limited
DK, One Embassy Gardens, 8 Viaduct Gardens,
London, SW11 7BW

The authorised representative in the EEA is
Dorling Kindersley Verlag GmbH. Arnulfstr. 124,
80636 Munich, Germany

Copyright © 2024 Dorling Kindersley Limited
A Penguin Random House Company
10 9 8 7 6 5 4 3 2 1
001–324970–Jan/2024

All rights reserved.
No part of this publication may be reproduced,
stored in or introduced into a retrieval system,
or transmitted, in any form, or by any means
(electronic, mechanical, photocopying, recording,
or otherwise), without the prior written permission
of the copyright owner.

A CIP catalogue record for this book
is available from the British Library.
ISBN: 978-0-2415-1517-4

Printed and bound in China

www.dk.com

THE AUTHOR AND CONSULTANT

Lizzie Munsey edits and writes books for children. She has worked in publishing for more than a decade, and has contributed to scores of books on a wide range of subjects, including space, science, natural history, geography, history, and maths. Her favourite number is 42. Lizzie lives in Oxford with her two children and two cats.

Dr Junaid Mubeen is a mathematician, writer, and educator. He has taught maths to students of all ages and abilities, from tots to University of Oxford graduates. Junaid believes there is a mathematician in all of us and relishes opportunities to show students new ways of understanding mathematical concepts. He once earned fame as series winner of the UK television game show *Countdown*.

CONTENTS

TICK WHEN COMPLETED!

- ☐ 4 **NUMBER SYMBOLS**
- ☐ 6 **PLACE VALUE**
- ☐ 8 **COMPARING NUMBERS**
- ☐ 10 **ADDITION**
- ☐ 12 **COLUMN ADDITION**
- ☐ 14 **SUBTRACTION**
- ☐ 16 **COLUMN SUBTRACTION**
- ☐ 18 **MULTIPLICATION**
- ☐ 20 **SHORT MULTIPLICATION**
- ☐ 22 **MULTIPLICATION TABLES**
- ☐ 24 **DIVISION**
- ☐ 26 **SHORT DIVISION**
- ☐ 28 **PARTITIONING**
- ☐ 30 **SEQUENCES**
- ☐ 32 **NEGATIVE NUMBERS**
- ☐ 34 **ESTIMATING AND ROUNDING**
- ☐ 36 **FRACTIONS**
- ☐ 38 **DECIMALS**
- ☐ 40 **PERCENTAGES**
- ☐ 42 **SCALING**
- ☐ 44 **MEASURING**

- ☐ 46 **PERIMETER**
- ☐ 48 **AREA**
- ☐ 50 **VOLUME**
- ☐ 52 **TIME**
- ☐ 54 **MONEY**
- ☐ 56 **LINES**
- ☐ 58 **ANGLES**
- ☐ 60 **TRIANGLES**
- ☐ 62 **QUADRILATERALS**
- ☐ 64 **POLYGONS**
- ☐ 66 **CIRCLES**
- ☐ 68 **3-D SHAPES**
- ☐ 70 **COORDINATES**
- ☐ 72 **TRANSFORMATIONS**
- ☐ 74 **SYMMETRY**
- ☐ 76 **COLLECTING DATA**
- ☐ 78 **GRAPHS AND CHARTS**
- ☐ 80 **MATHS QUIZ**
- ☐ 82 **MATHS IN NATURE**
- ☐ 84 **GLOSSARY**
- ☐ 86 **ANSWERS**

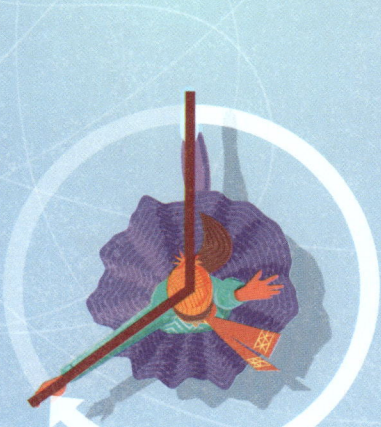

NUMBER SYMBOLS

Numbers have been written down for thousands of years. In ancient times, different number symbols were used across different parts of the world. Today, most people use a group of symbols called the Hindu-Arabic number system.

> THE NUMBER SYSTEM OF THE AMAZONIAN PIRAHÃ TRIBE IS MADE UP OF JUST FOUR WORDS: **ONE, TWO, FEW, AND MANY.**

Using number systems

Number systems allow you to describe different amounts by combining a set of symbols, following a fixed set of rules. These examples show how the numbers 1 to 10 can be written using different historical number systems.

	1	2	3	4	5	6	7	8	9	10
MODERN HINDU-ARABIC	1	2	3	4	5	6	7	8	9	10
MAYAN	•	••	•••	••••	—	•	••	•••	••••	=
CHINESE	一	二	三	四	五	六	七	八	九	十
ANCIENT ROMAN	I	II	III	IV	V	VI	VII	VIII	IX	X
ANCIENT EGYPTIAN										
BABYLONIAN										

Roman numerals

Ancient Romans used letters to represent numbers of different values. When numerals with the same value are written together, they are added. When a numeral with a smaller value appears before a bigger one, it is subtracted from the bigger numeral. If a numeral with a smaller value appears after a bigger one, it is added.

In the numeral IV, the 1 is subtracted from the 5, so IV means 4.

In the numeral VI, the 1 is added to the 5, so VI means 6.

I	II	III	IV	V	VI	VII
1	2	3	4	5	6	7
VIII	IX	X	XX	XXX	XL	L
8	9	10	20	30	40	50
LX	LXX	LXXX	XC	C	CC	CCC
60	70	80	90	100	200	300
CD	D	DC	DCC	DCCC	CM	M
400	500	600	700	800	900	1,000

Place value columns

To understand the value of each digit in a number, it can be helpful to imagine them in columns called place value columns. In a place value system, the smallest units represented are the ones, which are written on the right. Each position to the left of the ones makes the digit's value 10 times greater. Let's look at the digits in the number 2,037.

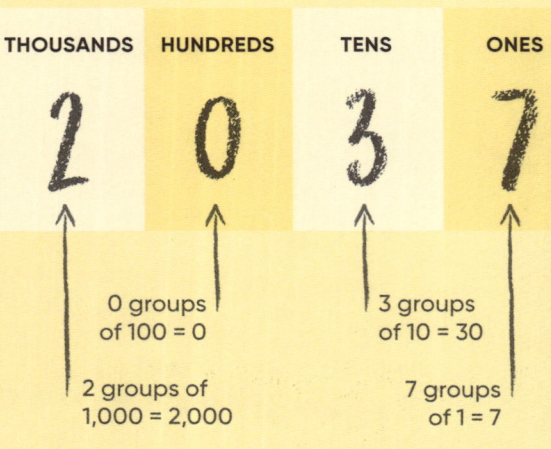

THE DECIMAL SYSTEM STARTED **ON OUR HANDS.** WE HAVE TEN FINGERS, SO WE COUNT IN **GROUPS OF TEN.**

PLACE VALUE

Our counting system is called the decimal system. The name comes from the Latin word for ten (*decem*) because it is based on thinking and counting in groups of 10. The system is made up of the ten digits 0 to 9, which vary in value depending on where in a number they are placed.

PUT THE NUMBERS IN THEIR PLACES

Can you work out the place value of each digit in the numbers below? Write the digits into the correct place value columns on this fence. We've done one for you.

5,611   ~~37~~   4   8,020   780

Th	H	T	O
....	....	3	7
....	....	....	....
....	....	....	....
....	....	....	....
....	....	....	....
....	....	....	....

WRITE IT!

WHOSE DOG?
These walkers have jumbled up their dogs. Use the descriptions to help you colour in each dog's coat to match the colour of its owner's speech bubble.

Four hundreds and six tens

Two thousands, five hundreds, and nine ones

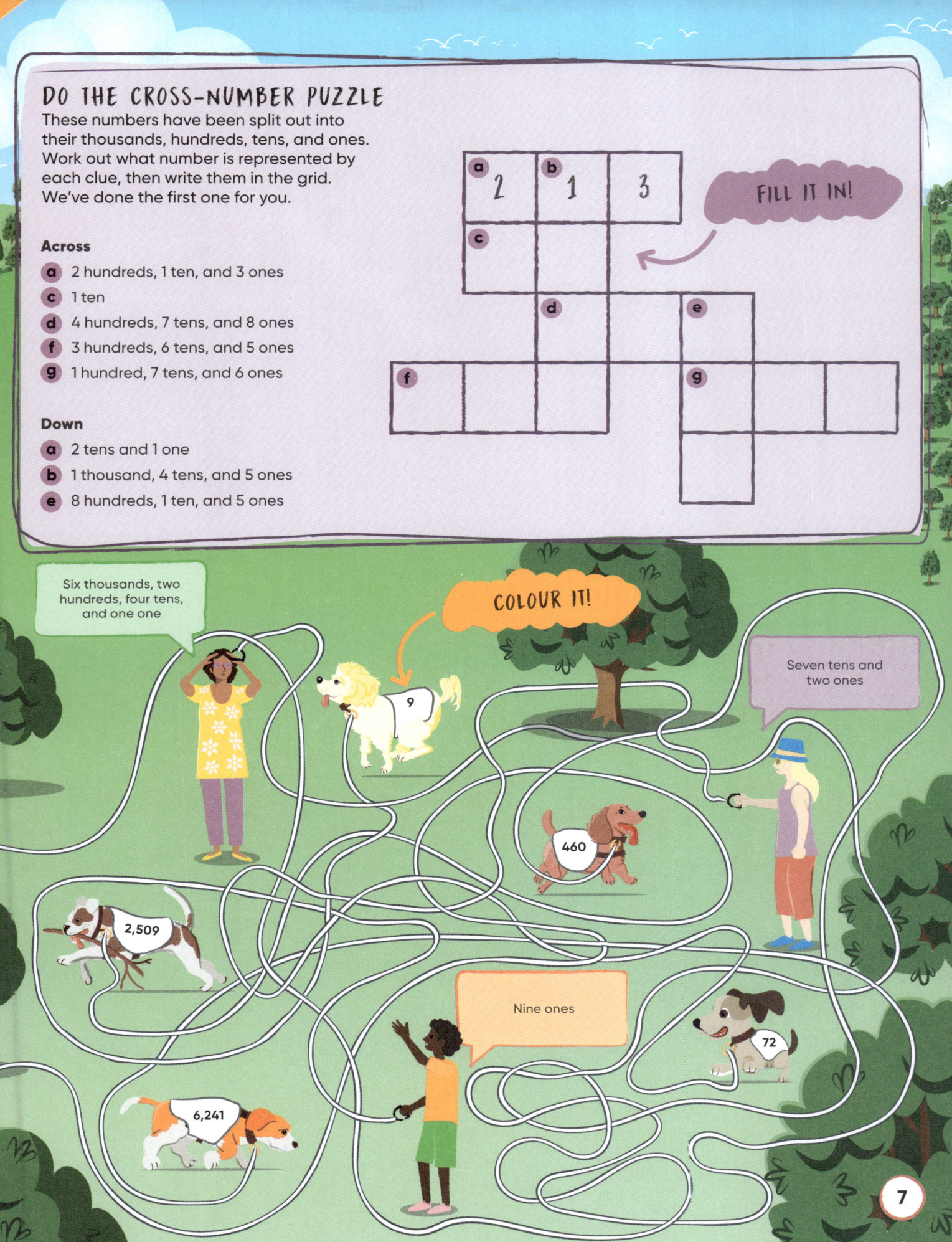

COMPARING NUMBERS

Sometimes it can be useful to know if one number or answer to a calculation is the same size as another, or if it is bigger or smaller. In maths, we can use a range of symbols to show the relationship between numbers.

WHICH WAY ROUND?
The wide, open end of a comparison arrow should always face the larger value. The closed, narrow end should face the smaller value.

Comparison symbols
There are three main comparison symbols we use in maths to compare numbers and amounts.

Greater than
This symbol is written between two numbers to show that the number to its left is greater than the number to its right. For example, 8 > 5 means "8 is greater than 5".

Less than
This symbol is written between two numbers to show that the number to its left is smaller than the number to its right. For example, 2 < 9 means "2 is less than 9".

Equal to
This symbol is written when the numbers or calculations shown on either side of it have the same value. For example, 1 + 3 = 4 means "1 + 3 is equal to 4".

WHICH SYMBOL?
Draw in the correct symbol to compare each of these pairs of numbers.

COMPARE IT!

a) 56 35
b) 42 42
c) 3 3
d) 6 88
e) 1 13
f) 71 23

MAKE IT TRUE
Write a comparison symbol to show the relationship between the number of gems on either side in each of the groups below.

WRITE IT!

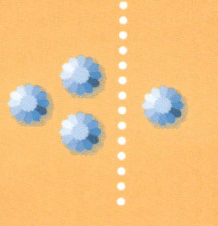

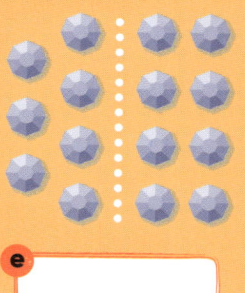

a ....
b ....
c ....
d ....
e ....

FIND THE WAY
There is just one path through each of these grids: one follows numbers less than 154, and the other follows numbers greater than 257. Use a green colouring pencil to colour your way across the grids. You can move up, down, left, and right, but not diagonally. We've coloured the first four for you.

COLOUR IT!

NUMBERS LESS THAN 154

137	348	673	398	208	589	EXIT	311
987	140	472	284	43	78	100	864
23	584	■	763	57	■	986	231
847	■	482	159	4	150	124	88
16	239	837	444	729	310	259	19
■	155	79	130	42	12	906	153
312	514	152	200	575	29	■	129
167	3	87	999	839	111	62	90
254	154	599	156	■	378	176	420

START ↑

NUMBERS GREATER THAN 257

807	200	EXIT	157	201	■	70	32
31	95	399	258	884	3	99	142
295	14	130	■	902	434	167	19
■	111	4	85	7	290	■	50
247	382	585	990	15	558	152	256
689	260	43	283	■	308	640	1
700	124	63	324	772	12	921	200
298	492	236	211	691	■	311	255
34	257	144	■	420	266	892	32

START ↑

ADDITION

Addition is a way to combine two or more numbers. We can think about addition in two different ways: counting up all the amounts that we are adding, and counting on from a bigger number by a smaller one. Both methods give the same answer.

WHAT ORDER?
Whichever order you choose to add the numbers in an addition calculation, the answer will be the same. For example, 2 + 4 = 6 and 4 + 2 = 6.

The addition sign
A plus sign (+) written between numbers tells us that the numbers should be added together.

3 + 2 = 5

This is the number we start with.

The plus sign shows we are doing addition.

This number is added on to the first number.

This symbol means "is equal to".

This is the answer or result, which is known as the "sum".

COUNT ALL THE BIRDS

One way to think about addition is as "counting all" – counting all the amounts you want to add. Count all the birds to find the answers to these calculations. We've done the first one for you.

ADD IT!

a) 2 + 4 = 6

b) ..... + ... + ... = ...

c) ..... + ... + ... = ...

COUNT ON

Another way to add is by "counting on". You start with the larger number in the addition and "count on" from that number in steps equal to the other number. Find the answer to each of these calculations using the number lines. We've done one for you.

COUNT IT!

a) 4 + 2 = ?   ......6......

b) 5 + 3 = ?   ......

c) 3 + 2 = ?   ......

FILL IN THE GAPS

Use what you have learned about addition to find the missing numbers in these sums. Use the space to draw out the fruits being added together to help you.

DRAW IT!

a)
5 + 6 = 11

b)
8 + ... = 12

c)
10 + ... = 14

d)
7 + 5 = ...

COLUMN ADDITION

Sometimes numbers are too big to be added together in your head, so it can be handy to know other methods to help you tackle tricky sums. Column addition is where we arrange the numbers in a sum into columns to help us add them up.

How to use column addition
In column addition, we write each number in the sum into columns and then add up the numbers in each column separately to give us the total. Let's use column addition to work out **291 + 34**.

BONUS QUESTION
Use column addition to add together the ages of the people in your family.

....

FIND FLYNN
Flynn is travelling around the world and has left this set of sums as a clue to where he's been. The answers to the sums match the longitude locations of six cities on the map on the right.

1. Find the answer to each column addition.

2. Work out which city each answer represents on the map, then write their names on the dotted line beside the correct letter.

HOW MANY DAYS?
Flynn has travelled for 47 days by aeroplane and 166 days by train on his trip around the world. Use column addition to work out the total number of days he has spent travelling.

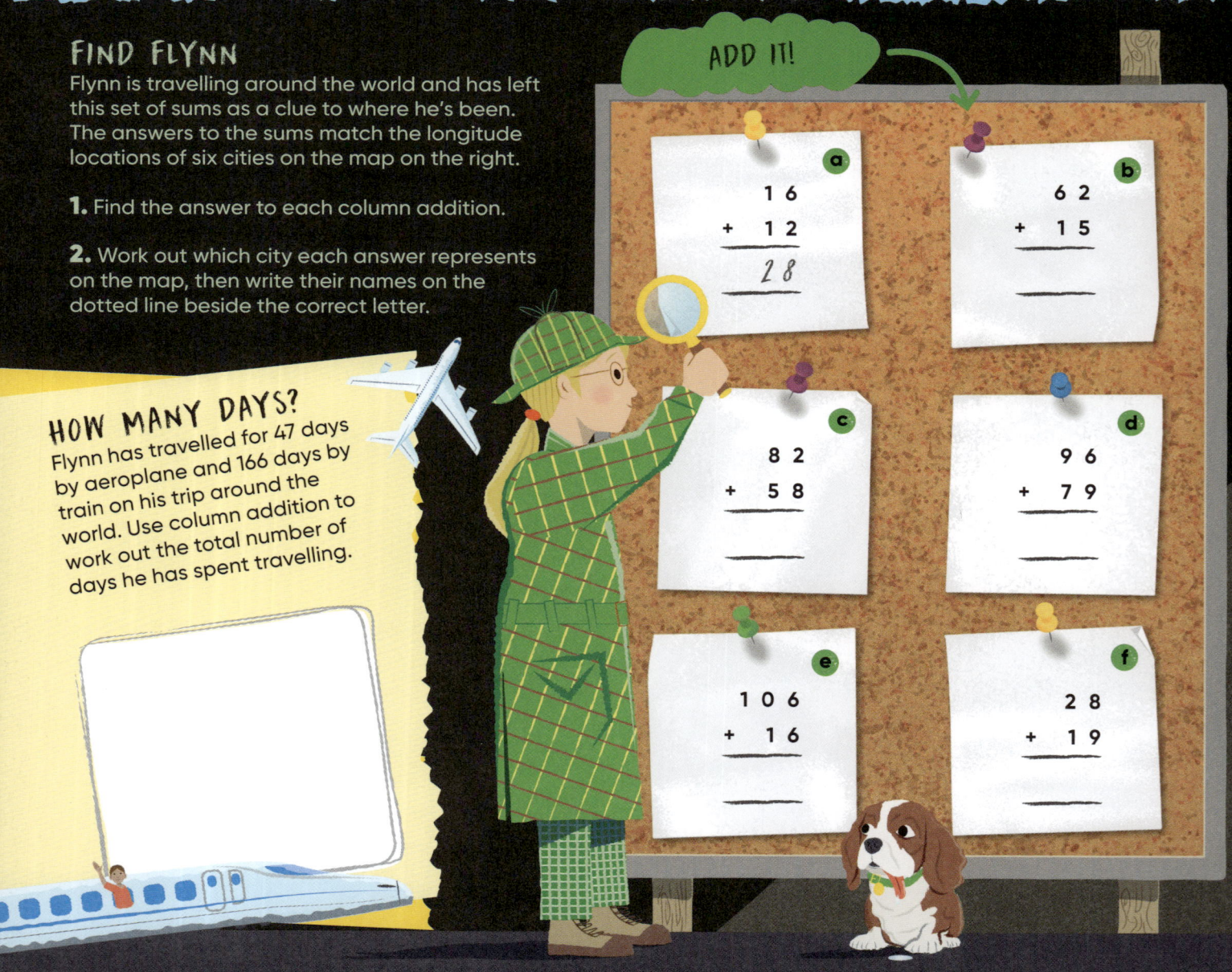

ADD IT!

a) 16 + 12 = 28

b) 62 + 15

c) 82 + 58

d) 96 + 79

e) 106 + 16

f) 28 + 19

Hundreds
Tens
Ones
H T O
2 9 1
+ 3 4
Add the ones first.
H T O
2 9 1
+ 3 4
5
H T O
2 9 1
+ 3 4
2 5
1
The 1 is "carried" to the next column.
H T O
2 9 1
+ 3 4
3 2 5
1

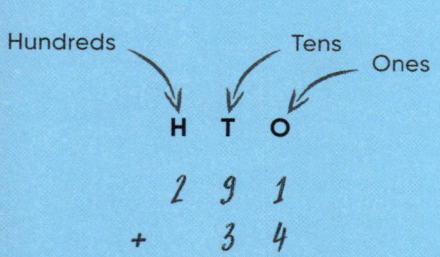

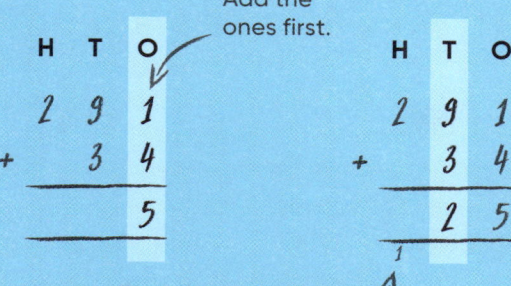

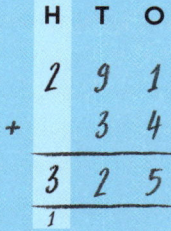

1 Write the numbers in columns, aligning digits that have the same place value. Write a **+** sign to the left and draw two lines below. You'll write your answer between the lines.

2 Add together the numbers in each of the columns, starting with the ones column: 1 + 4 = 5. Write 5 in the ones column between the lines.

3 Add the tens: 9 + 3 = 12. The total has two digits, so write the 2 between the lines in the tens column and "carry" the 1 to the hundreds column to add on later.

4 Finally, add the hundreds, including the carried digit from the previous stage: 2 + 1 = 3. Write the 3 between the lines in the hundreds column. So, **291 + 34 = 325**.

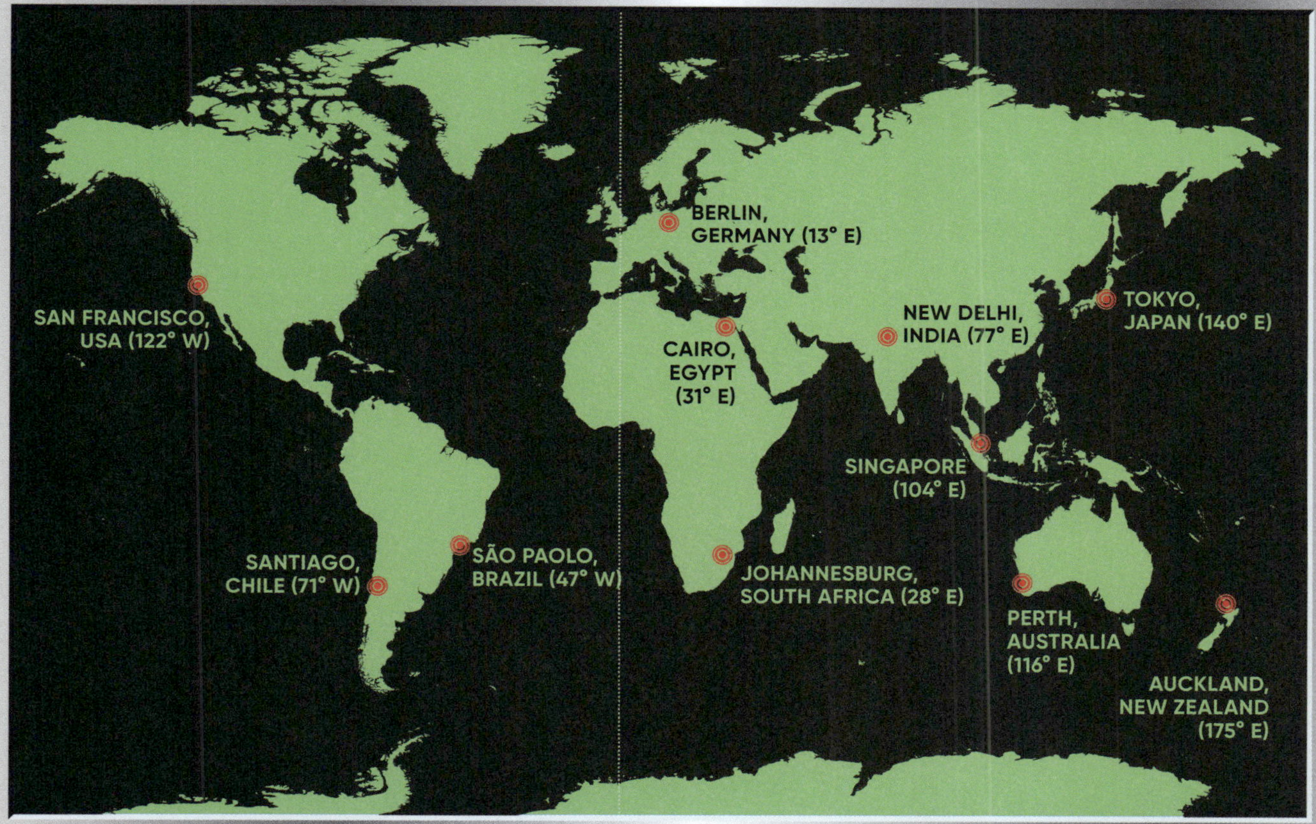

BERLIN, GERMANY (13° E)
SAN FRANCISCO, USA (122° W)
NEW DELHI, INDIA (77° E)
TOKYO, JAPAN (140° E)
CAIRO, EGYPT (31° E)
SINGAPORE (104° E)
SANTIAGO, CHILE (71° W)
SÃO PAOLO, BRAZIL (47° W)
JOHANNESBURG, SOUTH AFRICA (28° E)
PERTH, AUSTRALIA (116° E)
AUCKLAND, NEW ZEALAND (175° E)

a Johannesburg, South Africa
b ....
c ....
d ....
e ....
f ....

WRITE IT!

SUBTRACTION

Taking one number away from another number is called subtraction. We can think about subtraction in two different ways: as finding the difference between two numbers, or as taking away from a number by counting back from it. You will get the same answer whichever way you look at it.

THE RIGHT ORDER
You must subtract in the order numbers are written, or you will get the wrong answer. For example, 6 − 2 = 4 is correct, but 2 − 6 = 4 is not.

The subtraction sign
In a subtraction calculation, we use the minus sign (−) to show that one number is being subtracted from another. Unlike addition, the numbers in a subtraction must always be calculated in the order they are written.

5 − 3 = 2

This is the number being subtracted from.

The minus sign shows we are doing subtraction.

This is the number being subtracted.

This symbol means "is equal to".

This is the answer or result.

CIRCLE IT!

COUNT BACK
One way to look at subtraction is as counting back from the first number in a calculation in steps equal to the second number. Use the number lines to count back and solve these calculations, then circle the answers. We've done one for you.

8 − 2 =   0 1 2 3 4 5 6 7 8 9 10

5 − 3 =   0 1 2 3 4 5 6 7 8 9 10

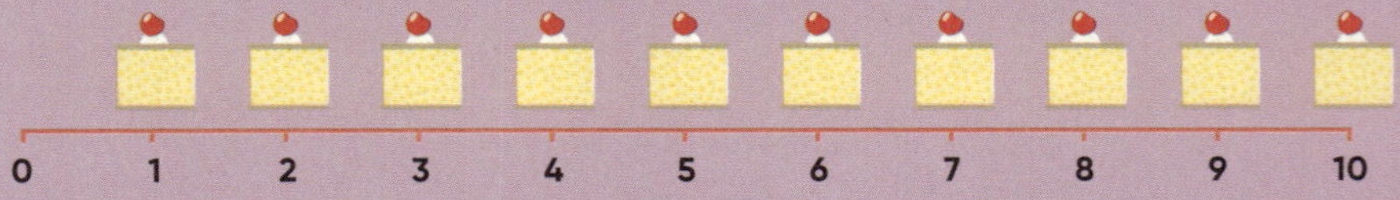

4 − 4 =   0 1 2 3 4 5 6 7 8 9 10

9 − 5 =   0 1 2 3 4 5 6 7 8 9 10

FIND THE DIFFERENCE

Subtraction can also be thought of as finding out how many steps it takes to get from the smaller number in a calculation to the larger number. Use the dials on the oven below to help you find the difference in these calculations. For each one, count the steps it takes to get from the smaller number to the larger one. We've done one for you.

DRAW IT!

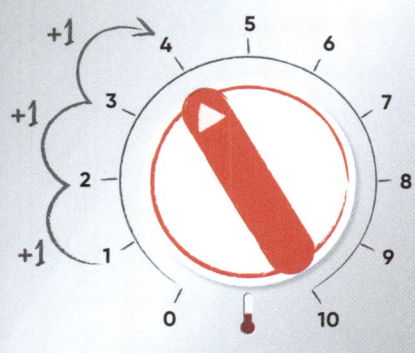

a 4 − 1 = 3

b 7 − 4 = ...

c 10 − 6 = ...

FILL IN THE GAPS

Use what you have learned about subtraction to help you find the missing numbers in these calculations. But watch out – some of them have more than one number to subtract! We've done the first one for you.

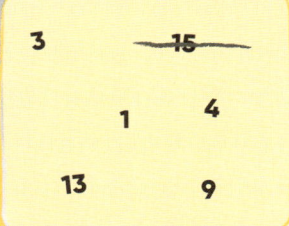

3   ~~15~~

       1   4

13   9

HOW MANY?

Fill in the answers to these subtraction word problems.

a Abdul bought 6 doughnuts, then ate 2. How many are left?

b A baker made 20 bread rolls. She sold 10, then ate 1 for her lunch. How many does she have left to sell?

c 2 loaves from a batch of 13 burned in the oven. How many loaves were not burned?

FILL IT IN!

a 20 − 5 = 15

b 17 − ...... − 2 = 6

c 12 − ...... = 8

d 13 − ...... = 10

e 18 − 2 − 3 = ...

f 7 − ...... − 2 = 4

WRITE IT!

COLUMN SUBTRACTION

When calculating with large numbers containing several digits, we can use a method called column subtraction to break the calculation up into smaller parts that are easier to work with.

How to use column subtraction
In column subtraction, we stack the numbers in the calculation so the place value of each digit matches. This method allows us to subtract the digits one at a time. Let's use column subtraction to find **314 − 172**.

1 Write the number being subtracted below the number it is being subtracted from, aligning digits with the same place value. Write a "−" sign to the left and draw two lines below. You'll write your answer between the lines.

2 Starting with the ones column, subtract the number on the bottom from the number on the top: 4 − 2 = 2. Write 2 between the lines in the ones column.

Subtract the ones.

3 Now, subtract the tens. If the bottom number is larger than the top, we "borrow" from the next column. Borrow 1 hundred (which is 10 tens) for a new total of 11 tens: 11 − 7 = 4. Write 4 between the lines.

The 3 in the hundreds column becomes 2. *1 hundred (10 tens) is borrowed.*

4 Finally, subtract the hundreds: 2 − 1 = 1. Write 1 between the lines in the hundreds column to reveal the final answer to the whole calculation: **314 − 172 = 142**.

FIND THE WAY
This monkey is trying to reach his friend, but needs help finding the right path. The answers to the subtraction sums match the numbers on some of the vines. Work out the answers, then colour in the vines to reveal the right ones for him to swing on.

MULTIPLICATION

Multiplying is a way of adding the same number or quantity to itself a certain number of times, like a repeated addition: 2 × 3 is the same as 2 + 2 + 2. If we think of multiplication as repeated addition, the first number in the calculation is the number to be added, and the second number is the number of times it should be added to itself.

YOU WILL GET THE SAME ANSWER WHICHEVER ORDER YOU MULTIPLY NUMBERS IN.

The multiplication sign
In a multiplication calculation, we use a multiplication sign (×) to show that numbers are being multiplied. It doesn't matter which way round you multiply numbers in a multiplication – the answer will always be the same.

We can picture the multiplication 4 × 3 as 3 rows of 4 watermelons.

We can picture 3 × 4 as 4 rows of 3 watermelons.

4 × 3 = 12

3 × 4 = 12

A multiplication sign shows we are multiplying the numbers.

The answer to a multiplication is called the "product".

These two numbers are being multiplied together.

MAKE A MULTIPLICATION
Can you change these repeated addition sums into multiplication calculations? Rewrite each one as a multiplication, then fill in the answers. We've done the first one for you.

WRITE IT!

4 + 4 + 4 = 12
a) 4 × 3 = 12

5 + 5 = ?
b) ...... × ...... = ...

2 + 2 + 2 + 2 = ?
c) ...... × ...... = ...

8 + 8 + 8 = ?
d) ...... × ...... = ...

18

The grid method

One way to solve a multiplication with larger numbers is the grid method. It works by breaking the numbers into smaller ones that are easier to work with, then adding the results together at the end. Let's see how it works with the calculation **6 × 14**.

14 is broken down into 10 and 4.

6 × 10 = 60

6 × 4 = 24

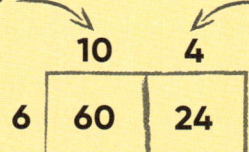

60 + 24 = 84

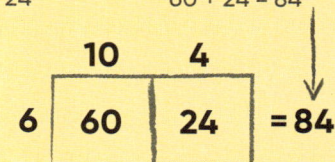

1 Draw a rectangle and label the short side with the smaller number from the calculation. Divide the box in half with a line.

2 Break the larger number into two numbers that are easier to work with and write them along the long side.

3 Multiply the number on the short side by each of the numbers on the long side, then write the answers in the boxes.

4 Add the answers in the two boxes together to find the answer to the multiplication calculation: **6 × 14 = 84**.

WORK IT OUT

Suraya has been hard at work in her garden, picking fruits and vegetables. How many has she picked of each? Look at each of the descriptions below and use the space provided to draw the items in rows and columns, called arrays. Use your array to help you write out each one as a multiplication calculation and fill in their answers.

a 5 GROUPS OF 6 RASPBERRIES

6 × 5 = 30

b 4 GROUPS OF 3 BEANS

....

c 3 GROUPS OF 10 PEAS

....

d 4 GROUPS OF 2 PUMPKINS

....

DRAW IT!

COMPLETE THE GRIDS

Have a go at using the grid method to solve each of these multiplication calculations. We've filled in some parts for you.

COMPLETE IT!

a 8 × 12 = ?   ____ 2
8 [|] = ...

b 4 × 71 = ?   4 [|] = ...

c 3 × 84 = ?   80 ____
3 [|] = ...

d 7 × 96 = ?   ____ 6
7 [|] = ...

SHORT MULTIPLICATION

Sometimes you might be faced with a multiplication calculation that's too tricky to work out in your head. But if you know your times tables, short multiplication is a method you can use to work through the problem. It involves breaking a tough calculation down into simpler parts.

COLLECT THE ANSWERS

Nikita's dog has run off with the answers to her maths homework and left them all over town! Solve each calculation below, then find your way through the maze to the right answers in any order to collect them. Write a, b, c, and d next to the correct answers. Beware of wrong answers and road blocks on the way!

a) 27 × 9
b) 812 × 6
c) 145 × 3
d) 49 × 2

How to use short multiplication

In short multiplication, we arrange the numbers from the calculation into columns, with digits that have the same place values stacked on top of each other.

A multiplication sign is written to the left.

```
   T O
   1 4
 ×   6
 ─────
```

"Carry" the 2 tens to below the tens column.

```
   T O
   1 4
 ×   6
 ─────
     4
   2
```

The total answer is 84.

```
   T O
   1 4
 ×   6
 ─────
   8 4
   2
```

1 Let's find 14 × 6. Write the larger number above the smaller one, with the tens digit in one column and the ones digits in another. Draw two lines underneath – you'll write the answer between the lines.

2 Multiply the ones digit in the top row by the number below: 4 × 6 = 24. Write the 4 in the ones column and the 2 below the answer box in the tens column to add on later. This is called carrying.

3 Next, multiply the tens in the top row by the same number as you did before: 1 × 6 = 6. Add the carried 2 from the previous calculation to your result: 6 + 2 = 8. Write 8 in the answer box. So, **14 × 6 = 84.**

FIND IT!

827   267   4,872
943
103   98

MULTIPLICATION TABLES

A multiplication table, or times table, is a list of the multiplication facts for a number. Knowing the times tables for all the numbers up to 12 can make it easier for you to perform many other, bigger calculations. The results you get from multiplying a number are known as its multiples. For example, 8, 12, and 16 are all multiples of 4.

×	1	2	3	4	5	6	7	8	9	10	11	12
1	1	2	3	4	5	6	7	8	9	10	11	12
2	2	4	6	8	10	12	14	16	18	20	22	24
3	3	6	9	12	15	18	21	24	27	30	33	36
4	4	8	12	16	20	24	28	32	36	40	44	48
5	5	10	15	20	25	30	35	40	45	50	55	60
6	6	12	18	24	30	36	42	48	54	60	66	72
7	7	14	21	28	35	42	49	56	63	70	77	84
8	8	16	24	32	40	48	56	64	72	80	88	96
9	9	18	27	36	45	54	63	72	81	90	99	108
10	10	20	30	40	50	60	70	80	90	100	110	120
11	11	22	33	44	55	66	77	88	99	110	121	132
12	12	24	36	48	60	72	84	96	108	120	132	144

The multiplication grid

This grid contains the values for all the times tables from 1 to 12. The answer to each calculation (called the product) is written in the square where the two numbers being multiplied meet. Two numbers can be multiplied either way round and you'll always get the same number. Here you can see that 6 × 9 has the same product as 9 × 6.

COLOUR THE MULTIPLES

This number square contains all the numbers from 1 to 100, in order. Use the key below to help you colour in the multiples of 2, 3, and 5 on the grid. Some of the squares will need to be coloured more than once!

Colouring key
- Multiples of 2
- Multiples of 3
- Multiples of 5

1	2	3	4	5	6	7	8	9	10
11	12	13	14	15	16	17	18	19	20
21	22	23	24	25	26	27	28	29	30
31	32	33	34	35	36	37	38	39	40
41	42	43	44	45	46	47	48	49	50
51	52	53	54	55	56	57	58	59	60
61	62	63	64	65	66	67	68	69	70
71	72	73	74	75	76	77	78	79	80
81	82	83	84	85	86	87	88	89	90
91	92	93	94	95	96	97	98	99	100

COLOUR IT!

ESCAPE THE CAVE

Uh oh! The path leading to the exit is booby-trapped! Help these explorers make their way out of the cave by working out the sums below, then circling the correct answers on the tiles. But be careful: if you get one wrong, they will fall into the lava below! We've done the first one for you.

a) 10 × 6 = 60
b) 9 × 9 = ...
c) 8 × 1 = ...
d) 7 × 11 = ...
e) 6 × 9 = ...
f) 5 × 5 = ...
g) 4 × 12 = ...
h) 3 × 7 = ...
i) 2 × 10 = ...
j) 1 × 3 = ...

CIRCLE IT!

PRIME NUMBERS
Some whole numbers cannot be exactly divided by any whole numbers except 1 and themselves. These are called prime numbers. 2, 3, 5, 7, and 11 are the first five prime numbers.

DIVISION

Splitting a number into equal parts or groups is called division. Dividing can show us how many times one number fits into another, or how many equal parts an amount can be split into.

The division sign
In a calculation, we use the division sign (÷) to show that one number is being divided by another. Unlike multiplication, which you can perform in any order, division must be performed in the order the numbers are written out.

REMAINDERS
Sometimes a number won't divide by another exactly. For example, 9 ÷ 4 leaves 1 left over. Parts that are left over are called remainders.

15 ÷ 3 = 5

- The dividend is the number that will be divided.
- The division sign shows we are doing division.
- The divisor is how many parts the dividend will be divided into.
- The answer, or quotient, shows the size of each part.

SHARE OUT THE FLOWERS
Divide the flowers into groups to find the answers to these division calculations. Use the pictures to help you work them out. Tip: dividing a number by itself equals 1.

SHARE IT OUT!

(a) 9 ÷ 3 = 3

(b) 4 ÷ 4 = ...

(c) 12 ÷ 6 = ...

(d) 20 ÷ 5 = ...

MATCH THE CALCULATIONS

Division is the opposite of multiplication. For example, if you know that 5 × 2 = 10, then you also know that 10 ÷ 2 = 5 and that 10 ÷ 5 = 2. Each of these bunches has a multiplication calculation. Colour in the two matching division calculations for each one.

3 × 5 = 15   2 × 7 = 14   4 × 6 = 24

15 ÷ 3 = 5   24 ÷ 4 = 6   14 ÷ 7 = 2   15 ÷ 5 = 3   14 ÷ 2 = 7   24 ÷ 6 = 4

COLOUR IT!

UNSCRAMBLE THE WORDS

The names for the parts of a division calculation have been mixed up. Unscramble the letters and write the names into the spaces below.

V I D D I D E N

a

U T Q I O N T E

b

UNSCRAMBLE IT!

HOW MANY FLOWERS IN A BUNCH?

Lei is picking flowers to divide between herself and her two friends. How many will each person get of each type of flower? Once you have divided up all the flowers, draw Lei's bunch in the vase.

DRAW IT!

6 DAFFODILS

a   6 ÷ 3 = 2

3 SUNFLOWERS

b   .... ÷ 3 = ...

9 TULIPS

c   .... ÷ 3 = ...

12 ROSES

d   .... ÷ 3 = ...

DIVIDE IT!

SHORT DIVISION

If you know your times tables, you can probably do many division calculations up to dividing by 12 in your head. Short division is a written method you can use instead when the numbers are too large or when one number won't divide perfectly into another number.

PREPARE THE POTION
Can you help this wizard make his potion? Complete each calculation below to reveal the ingredients, then write them on the maths potion recipe sheet and draw them in the cauldron. We've done the first one for you.

How to use short division
In short division, you divide a large number by a single-digit number by working through the large number one digit at a time. The number you are dividing is called the dividend and the number being divided by is called the divisor. Let's use short division to find out the answer to **126 ÷ 4**.

1 Draw a bracket in the shape of a letter L on its side, like the one shown here. Write the dividend under the bracket and the divisor to the left of the bracket.

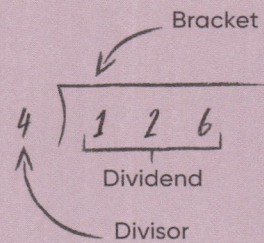

2 Divide each digit of the dividend, starting with the hundreds. 1 can't be divided by 4, so the space above the bracket is left empty and the 1 hundred is carried over into the next column.

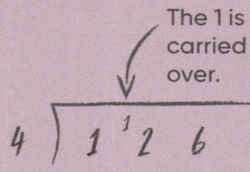

3 Now look at the tens. 1 hundred from the previous step was carried over, so instead of 2 tens we have 12 tens. Divide the tens by the divisor and write the answer above the bracket: 12 ÷ 4 = 3.

4 Look at the ones: 6 ÷ 4 = 1 with 2 left over. If a number does not divide exactly into another, the amount left over is called a remainder (r). Write 1 above the bracket, and "r 2" next to it. So, **126 ÷ 4 = 31 r2**.

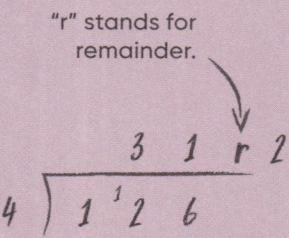

Secret recipe

a) 4) 5 1 2   (answer: 1 3)

b) 2) 1 2 4

c) 5) 3 6 5

d) 6) 7 3 8

e) 3) 1 9 8

Ingredients
5. Mistletoe berries
13. Toenails
43. Pansy pollen
55. Ogre nose hair
62. Oak bark
66. Mouldy apple
70. Grated silver
73. Earwax
96. Goblin snot
102. Raven's feather
115. Frog poo
123. Sweaty sock

26

COLOUR-BY-REMAINDERS

The answer to each of the division calculations in this picture has a remainder. Work out the answers on a piece of paper, then colour each section according to the key below.

Colouring key
- Remainder 1
- Remainder 2
- Remainder 3
- Remainder 4
- Remainder 5

COLOUR IT!

$106 \div 3$
$101 \div 7$
$59 \div 5$
$149 \div 6$
$46 \div 3$
$173 \div 3$
$83 \div 5$

BONUS QUESTION
The wizard needs to divide his potion into 8 bottles. If he has 752 ml of potion, how many ml of potion will be in each bottle?

....

Maths potion recipe
Toenails
a ....
b ....
c ....
d ....
e ....

WRITE IT!

DRAW IT!

PARTITIONING

It's important to learn the standard written methods for addition, subtraction, multiplication, and division calculations. However, knowing some simple tricks can help you find answers to calculations more quickly and easily, especially if you need to do them in your head. Partitioning is a method that breaks calculations into chunks to help you solve them.

What is partitioning?
Partitioning is simply breaking a number down by place value to make it simpler to work with. For example, 87 is a tricky number to perform a calculation with. If we break the number down into its tens and ones, giving us the numbers 80 and 7, we can perform calculations much more easily.

87
↙ ↘
80   7

How to use partitioning
If you are faced with a calculation that involves big or tricky numbers that you need to do in your head, you can use partitioning to help you solve it. Once you've partitioned the numbers into their tens and ones, you can do calculations with the smaller numbers, then add them back together in stages. Let's use partitioning to add together 62 and 35.

1 Partition 62 and 35 into their tens and ones.
60, 2, 30, 5

2 Add together the tens and ones separately.
60 + 30 = 90
2 + 5 = 7

3 Add together the two results to give you the total.
90 + 7 = 97

BONUS QUESTION
There were 56 people in the park, then 27 more arrived. Use partitioning to find the total number of people.
....

ADDING
Can you use partitioning to solve these addition calculations? We've filled in some of the steps for you.

a) 21 + 18 = ?

| T O | | T O | | T O |
| 2 0 | + | 1 0 | = | 3 0 |

| T O | | T O | | T O |
| 1 .. | + | .. 8 | = | .. 9 |

| T O |
| 3 9 |

b) 67 + 31 = ?

| T O | | T O | | T O |
| .. .. | + | 3 0 | = | 9 0 |

| T O | | T O | | T O |
| .. 7 | + | .. .. | = | .. 8 |

| T O |
| .. .. |

c) 39 + 28 = ?

| T O | | T O | | T O |
| .. .. | + | 2 0 | = | 5 .. |

| T O | | T O | | T O |
| .. 9 | + | .. 8 | = | .. .. |

| T O |
| .. .. |

ADD IT!

SUBTRACTING

When subtracting, we usually only partition the number being subtracted – its tens are taken away first, followed by its ones. Solve the four coloured subtraction problems by drawing an arrow from each one to each of its parts in order, then colouring in the parts to match their question. We've done one for you.

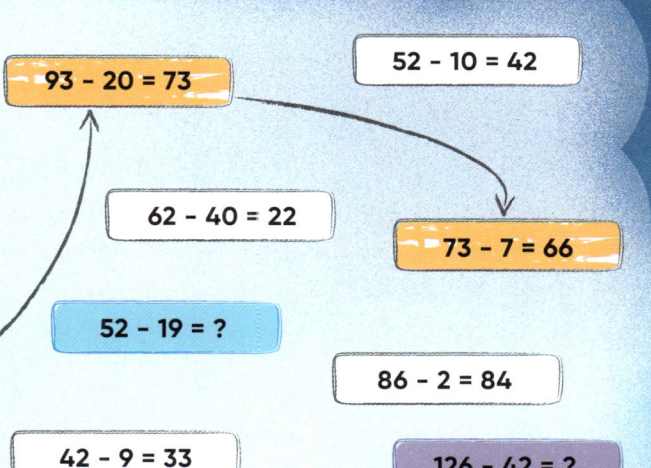

93 − 20 = 73
52 − 10 = 42
62 − 40 = 22
73 − 7 = 66
52 − 19 = ?
86 − 2 = 84
42 − 9 = 33
126 − 42 = ?
93 − 27 = ?
126 − 40 = 86
22 − 5 = 17
62 − 45 = ?

SUBTRACT IT!

MULTIPLYING

When multiplying, we partition the larger number. The other number in the calculation is multiplied by each of the parts, and then the totals are added together. Use partitioning to complete these multiplications.

a 13 × 9 = ?

10 × 9 = 90
3 × 9 = 27
90 + 27 = 117

b 24 × 6 = ?

20 × .... = ...
.... × 6 = ...
.... + ... = ...

c 37 × 4 = ?

.... × 4 = ...
7 × .... = ...
.... + ... = ...

MULTIPLY IT!

DIVIDING

To divide, we partition the number that is being divided. The division is done for each part, then the two answers are added together. Complete this partitioned division.

125 ÷ 5 = ?

125

100   25

100 ÷ 5 = ...   25 ÷ 5 = ...

.... + ... = ...

125 ÷ 5 = ...

DIVIDE IT!

SEQUENCES

A series of numbers or shapes that follows a set pattern is called a sequence. Each number in a sequence is called a term, and the set pattern they follow is called a rule.

Finding patterns
If you can work out the rule a sequence follows, you can continue the sequence. There are many ways to make a sequence, for example by adding or multiplying numbers, or even rotating shapes.

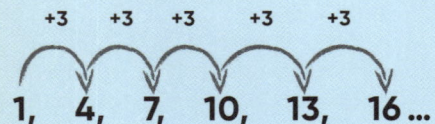

RULE: ADD 3

1, 4, 7, 10, 13, 16 …

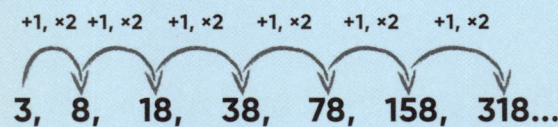

RULE: ADD 1 AND MULTIPLY BY 2

3, 8, 18, 38, 78, 158, 318 …

RULE: A REPEATING SEQUENCE OF 3 SHAPES

SEQUENCES DON'T ALWAYS HAVE TO START WITH 1 – THEY CAN BEGIN WITH ANY NUMBER OR SHAPE.

CONTINUE THE SEQUENCES

Look at these sequences and work out what rule they are following. Then write or draw in four terms that would continue each sequence.

 WRITE IT!

a) 2, 4, 6, 8, ….. , ….. , ….. , …..

b)  ….. ….. ….. …..

c) 90, 80, 70, 60, ….. , ….. , ….. , …..

d) ↑ → ↓ ← ….. ….. ….. …..

e)  ….. ….. ….. …..

f) 1, 2, 4, 7, 11, ….. , ….. , ….. , …..

The Fibonacci sequence

This special sequence is named after a 13th-century Italian mathematician. The first two numbers in the sequence are 1 and 1. Each number that follows is the sum of the two numbers that came before it.

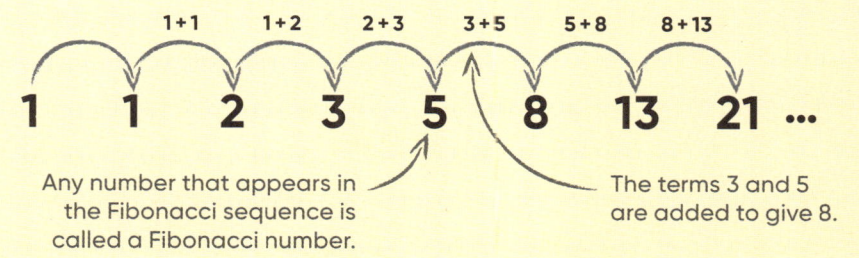

Any number that appears in the Fibonacci sequence is called a Fibonacci number.

The terms 3 and 5 are added to give 8.

WHAT ARE SQUARE NUMBERS?

A whole number multiplied by itself is called a square number. The sequence of square numbers can be drawn as squares, where each side is the length of the number that has been squared. Use the grid paper to help you draw the sequence of squared numbers.

DRAW IT!

a $1 \times 1 =$ ....1....

b $2 \times 2 =$ ....4....

c $3 \times 3 =$ ....

d $4 \times 4 =$ ....

e $5 \times 5 =$ ....

DRAW A FIBONACCI SPIRAL

The Fibonacci sequence can be used to draw a spiral shape. You start by drawing squares with sides the length of the sequence terms. Each square is drawn next to the last, working in an anticlockwise direction. Then you join the corners of each square with a curved line. This Fibonacci spiral shape can be seen throughout nature, from twisting hurricanes to spiral seashells. Join the dots below to complete the Fibonacci spiral.

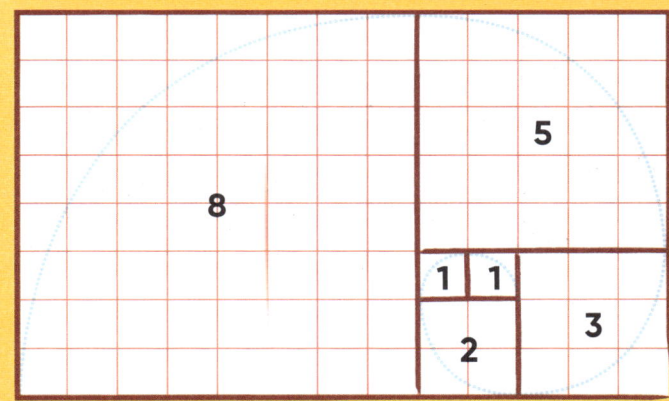

DRAW IT!

Fibonacci spirals can be seen in seashells

BONUS QUESTION

Can you find Fibonacci numbers and spirals in nature? Count the petals on flowers and spot spirals in shells and sunflower heads.

NEGATIVE NUMBERS

Not all numbers refer to quantities that are greater than zero. Some numbers, called negative numbers, have a value that is less than zero. They are useful for describing things like amounts of money owed, distances below sea level, and very chilly temperatures.

A minus sign tells us this number is negative (less than zero).

Negative numbers count down from zero.

–4 –3 –2 –1 0

Zero is neither positive nor negative.

What are negative numbers?
All numbers greater than zero are called positive numbers, while numbers with a value less than zero are called negative numbers. Just like with positive numbers, you can count negative numbers from zero, but in the opposite direction. We show a number is negative by writing a minus sign in front of it.

POSITIVE OR NEGATIVE?
Counting with negative numbers on a number line works just the same as positive numbers: you simply move left to count down and right to count up. What number do you get to when you count up and down on these number lines? We've done the first one for you.

WRITE IT!

a Count down 5 from 0 → -5

b Count up 2 from –3 → .....

c Count up 6 from –4 → .....

d Count down 3 from –1 → .....

COUNTING BACK THROUGH HISTORY
The use of negative numbers dates back to ancient China, where merchants kept track of their money using red (positive) and black (negative) rods.

Positive numbers count up from zero.

On a standard number line, negative numbers appear to the left of zero and positive numbers to the right.

HOW DEEP?
Negative numbers can be used to measure a distance below the surface of water, such as the surface of the sea or the depth of this pool.

1. Some of the numbers are missing from the height scale below. Fill in the missing numbers and remember to include a minus symbol for negative numbers.

2. How far is it to the bottom of the pool from the diving board? Write your answer in the square box below.

COMPLETE IT!

ROLL UP! ROLL UP!
Money can be expressed in negative amounts. If the circus made £80 from selling tickets and paid £110 to the performers, how much money would they be left with? Use the number line to help you.
Tip: start at zero and count up for the money made, then down for the money spent.

CIRCLE IT!

WRITE IT!

ESTIMATING AND ROUNDING

It's not always easy to calculate something on the spot, especially if the numbers are so large or tricky that they can't be easily calculated. Sometimes it is useful to work out a rough answer instead, without needing to precisely count or calculate it. We do this by using estimation and rounding.

ROUGHLY EQUAL
When writing an answer you have estimated, you can use a ≈ sign. This sign means "approximately equal to" and tells us the answer is not exact.

HOW BUSY IS THE BEACH?

It must be the school holidays, because the beach is very busy! Choose one of the methods at the top of the next page to estimate the number of parasols, then write your answer in the box below.

WRITE IT!

BONUS QUESTION
Count the parasols one by one to find out the actual number. How many parasols are there?

34

Estimating an amount

When you have a group of things that would take a long time to count or calculate exactly, you can roughly work out how many there are. This is called estimating. Let's estimate the number of shells on this beach.

Using columns or rows
Divide the area into approximate columns and count how many shells there are in one column. Multiply that number by the total number of columns: **8 × 8 = 64**. This estimation is very close the real number, 63.

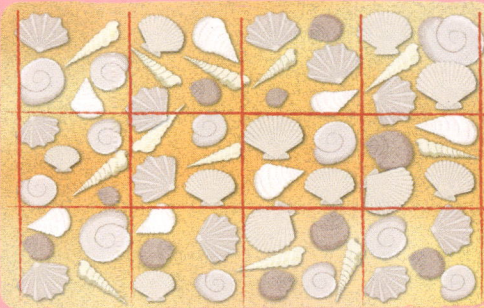

Using a grid
You can also estimate by dividing the area into a grid. Count the shells in one section, then multiply that number by the total number of sections in the grid: **5 × 12 = 60**. This is close to the actual number, 63.

Rounding numbers

Rounding involves changing numbers to other numbers that are similar in size, but simpler to work with. This can be useful if you have a tricky calculation to work out. Numbers can be rounded up or down, or to different place values, such as the nearest 1, 10, or 100. Rounding can also be useful to check if your answer to a calculation is roughly correct.

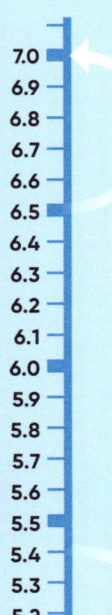

If the last digit is **5 or higher**, the number is rounded up. So, 6.5 is rounded up to 7.

If the last digit is **less than 5**, the number is rounded down. So, 5.4 is rounded down to 5.

HOW MUCH WILL IT COST?

You need to buy one of each type of ice cream to share among your friends, but the numbers aren't that easy to work with. Round each of the prices up or down to the nearest pound, then add them together to work out roughly how much money the ice creams will cost in total.

ROUND IT!

£1.00 a
+ ...... b
+ c
+ ...... d
= ......

FRACTIONS

There are many reasons why we might need to divide something into equal smaller parts or groups, such as sharing out a pie, pizza, or bag of sweets to make sure everyone gets the same amount. Fractions are a way of writing how much of one single thing or a group of things we're talking about.

Writing fractions
A fraction is written as one number on top of another, with a line between them. The bottom number (called the denominator) tells us how many parts a whole thing has been divided into or how many things there are in a group. The top number (called the numerator) tells us how many parts of the whole group we have.

 We have 3 parts.

$$\frac{3}{4}$$

 The whole is divided into 4 equal parts.

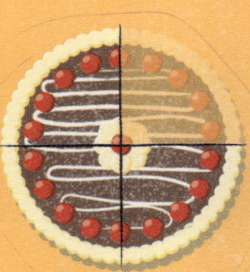

A fraction of a whole
¼ of this whole cake has been eaten and ¾ is left.

A fraction of a group
¼ of this group of cherries have been eaten and ¾ are left.

 WRITE IT!

WHAT FRACTION?
This lunchbox is full of yummy food. Fill in the boxes to show what fraction of each food the arrows are pointing to. Use the fractions from the box below. Remember: the total number of parts goes below the line, and the number of parts you have goes above the line. We've done the first one for you.

½   4/5   5   9/10   8   3/7

Equivalent fractions

A single fraction can be written in different ways. For example, 6/8 of the pizza below is exactly the same amount as 3/4. These are called equivalent fractions. To make an equivalent fraction, we simply multiply or divide the top and bottom numbers of a fraction by the same value, for example 2.

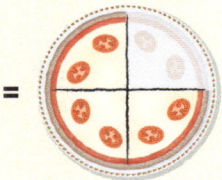

$$\frac{6}{8} = \frac{3}{4}$$

DRAW IT!

ADD THE TOPPINGS

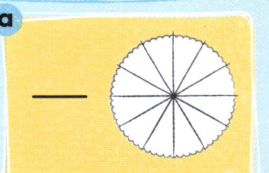

Everyone has their favourite pizza toppings. Look at the fractions for each of the toppings below and draw them on the correct number of pizza slices on the right. Tip: each slice can have more than one type of topping.

$$\frac{3}{4} \qquad \frac{7}{8} \qquad \frac{1}{2} \qquad \frac{1}{4} \qquad \frac{5}{8}$$

COMPLETE IT!

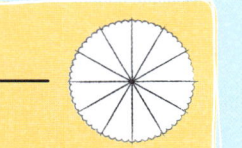

COMPLETE THE PIE

Complete this grid by writing in the missing fractions. The fractions in each row and each column should add up to a whole pie in total (12/12). The answers you will need are given below.

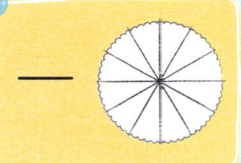

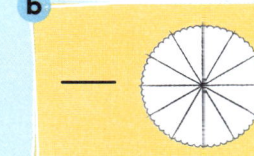

5/12	1/12	a. ___
6/12	b. ___	4/12
c. ___	9/12	2/12

$$\frac{2}{12} \qquad \frac{6}{12} \qquad \frac{1}{12}$$

DECIMALS

Decimals are a way of writing numbers and parts of numbers very accurately. They allow us to show much smaller parts of a number than we can with whole numbers, such as parts of a metre in sports. Decimal numbers are shown using a decimal point.

TEN TIMES SMALLER
The word "decimal" comes from the Latin word for "ten". In a decimal number, each digit on the right of the decimal point is 10 times smaller than the one to the left of it.

Tenths and hundredths
In decimal numbers, whole numbers are separated from parts of numbers using a dot, called a decimal point. Each digit after a decimal point represents increasingly smaller parts of a number, starting with tenths, then hundredths, and so on.

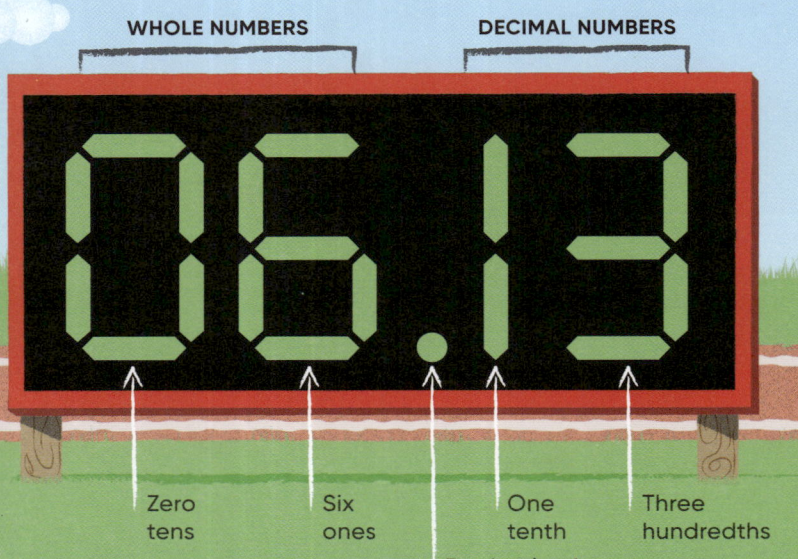

WHOLE NUMBERS | **DECIMAL NUMBERS**

06.13

- Zero tens
- Six ones
- Decimal point
- One tenth
- Three hundredths

WHO'S THE WINNER?
Can you put the shot put distances in order from biggest to smallest? To work out the correct order, compare the value of each digit in the numbers, starting with the highest place value. We've done the first one for you.

9.58 m
9.90 m
9.72 m
~~10.27 m~~
10.03 m

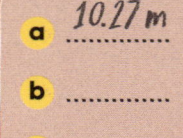

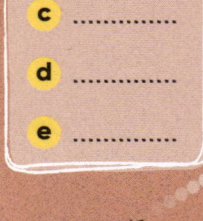

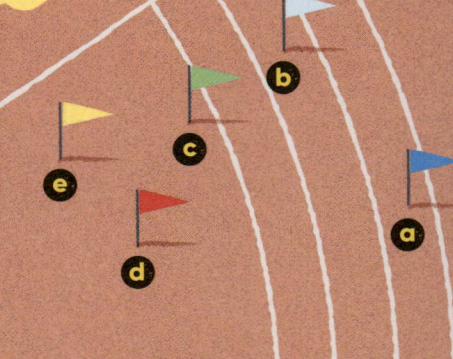

WRITE IT!

a. 10.27 m
b. ....
c. ....
d. ....
e. ....

COLOUR-BY-DECIMALS

Use the key below to help you colour the sections of this picture. There are different colours for whole numbers, numbers with tenths, numbers with hundredths, and numbers with thousandths.

Colouring key
- Whole numbers
- Numbers with tenths
- Numbers with hundredths
- Numbers with thousandths

COLOUR IT!

MOVE THE DECIMAL POINT

When you multiply or divide a decimal by 10 or 100, you simply shift the decimal point left or right. Use the rules below to help you work out the answer to each of these calculations. We've done two for you.

Rules

× 10: One place to right ÷ 10: One place to left
× 100: Two places to right ÷ 100: Two places to left

a 14.85 × 10 = 148.5

b 76.24 ÷ 10 = 7.624

c 62.31 × 10 = ...

d 329.1 ÷ 10 = ...

e 9.149 × 100 = ...

f 511.2 ÷ 100 = ...

WORK IT OUT!

FIND THE FRACTIONS

Fractions and decimals are both ways of writing proportions of numbers. Draw lines to match up these common decimals to their fraction equivalents. Use the two answers that have been given to help you work out the rest.

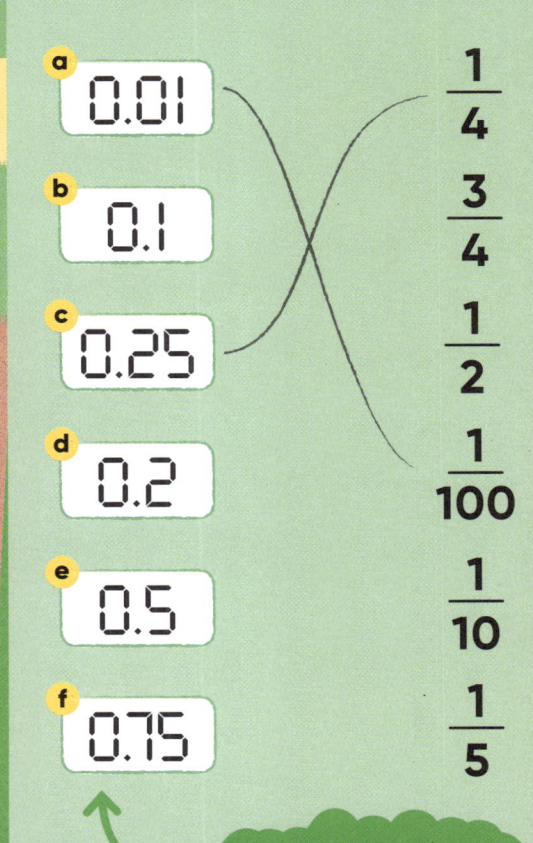

a 0.01
b 0.1
c 0.25
d 0.2
e 0.5
f 0.75

$\frac{1}{4}$
$\frac{3}{4}$
$\frac{1}{2}$
$\frac{1}{100}$
$\frac{1}{10}$
$\frac{1}{5}$

MATCH IT!

PERCENTAGES

The word "percentage" or "per cent" means "out of a hundred". In maths, we use percentages to describe parts of a whole, like how we use fractions. With percentages, a thing or group of things is thought of as being made up of 100 equal parts. We use a number and the symbol "%" to describe a percentage of the whole amount.

Parts of 100

The easiest way to understand a percentage is to imagine a block of 100 units, where each unit is equivalent to 1% of the total. If you have 25%, you have 25 out of the total 100 units. This can also be written as the fraction 25/100.

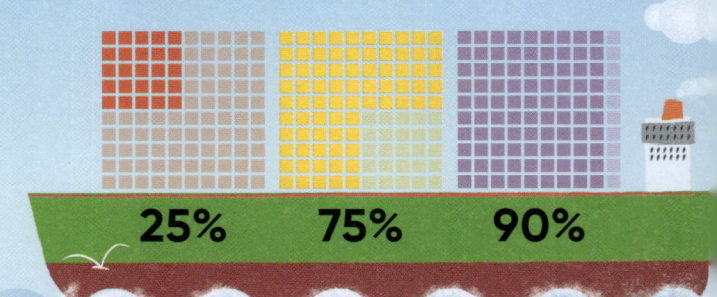

25%   75%   90%

FILL IN THE FISH

There are five different types of fish swimming in this shoal of 100 fish. Use the key to colour the correct percentage of each type.

Colouring key
- 50%
- 10%
- 25%
- 3%
- 12%

COLOUR IT!

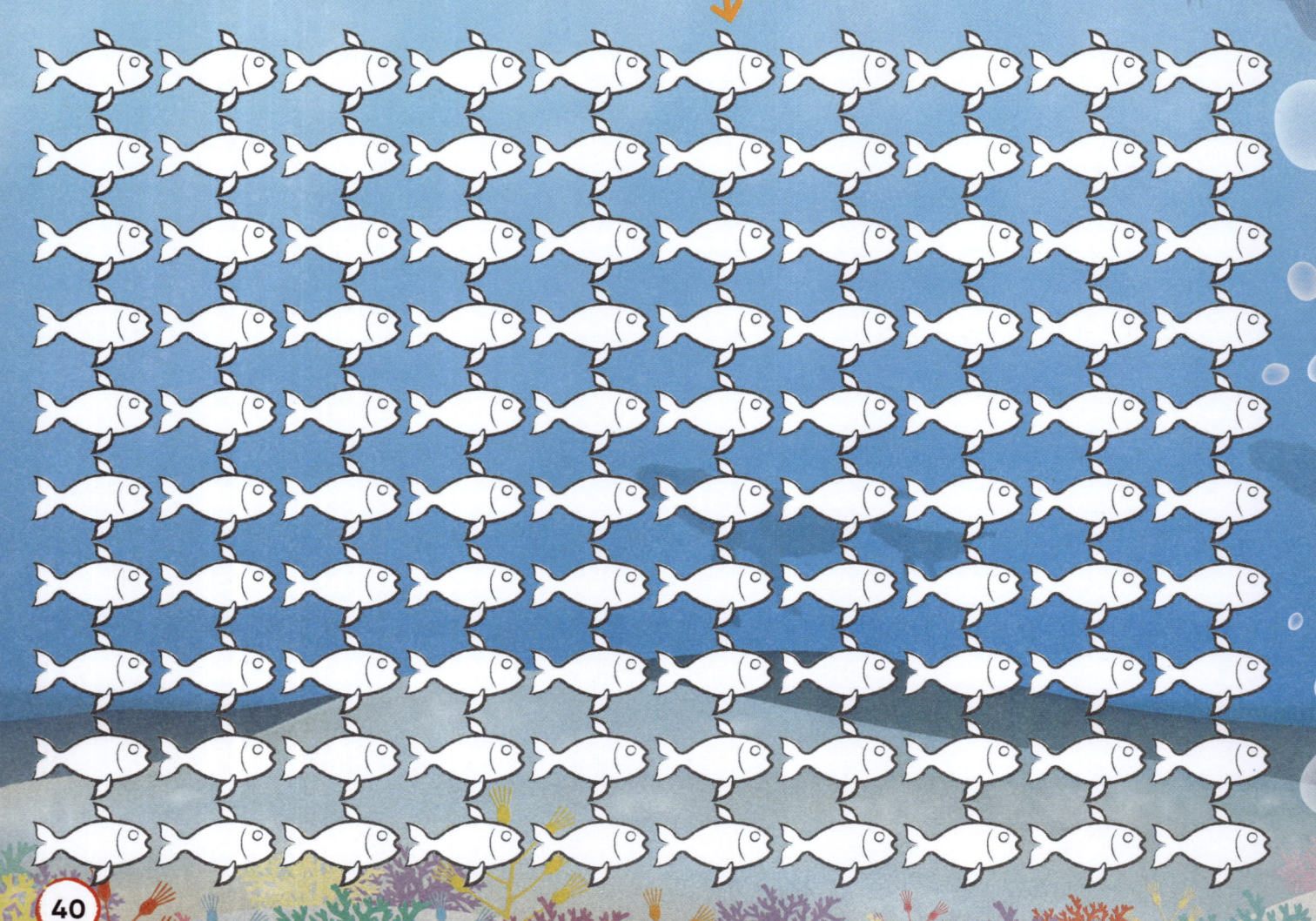

WHAT PERCENTAGE?

Percentages don't just have to describe a group of 100 things. They can also be used to describe a share of a whole or a group, but expressed as a part of 100. Draw a line to match the percentage of each group that is highlighted in these pictures.

PARTS OF A LIFEBELT   CRABS   DIVERS

This lifebelt has 10 parts, so each part is worth 10%. 2 parts are equal to 20%, so 20% is highlighted.

80%   20%   50%

MATCH IT!

FIND THE TREASURE

Work out these percentages and then colour the correct answers to help the divers make it safely through these bubbles to reach the treasure chest.

Start

50

15%

UH OH! SHARK APPROACHING – GO BACK TO THE START.

WHAT IS 10% OF 100?

100

10

WHAT PERCENTAGE OF 200 IS 50?

20%

WHAT IS 50% OF 50?

WHAT PERCENTAGE OF 100 IS 20?

25%

5

16

25

15%

WHAT IS 80% OF 20?

Finish

YOUR SCUBA TANK IS EMPTY – GO BACK TO THE START.

15

FIND IT!

SCALING

Making something bigger or smaller while keeping everything in proportion is called scaling. "In proportion" means that all the sizes are changed by the same amount.

Scale factors
Scaling up or down is done by multiplying by a number called a scale factor. If the scale factor is larger than 1, the shape is made bigger. If it is smaller than 1, the shape is made smaller.

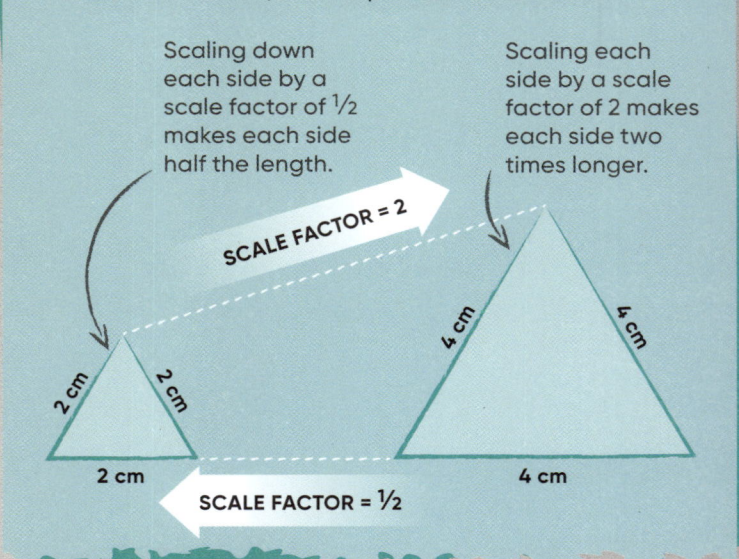

Scaling down each side by a scale factor of ½ makes each side half the length.

Scaling each side by a scale factor of 2 makes each side two times longer.

SCALE FACTOR = 2

SCALE FACTOR = ½

Resize the objects
Shapes, objects, quantities, and measurements can all be scaled up and down. This inventor is using his resizing machine on some of the objects in his workshop to make them bigger and smaller. Can you work out the size that each object will end up when they are scaled by the scale factors given below? We've done the first one for you.

WRITE IT!

a. 20 cm — 100 cm — SCALE FACTOR = ⅕

b. .... cm — 70 cm — SCALE FACTOR = 10

c. .... cm — 15 cm — SCALE FACTOR = 20

SCALE A ROOM IN YOUR HOUSE

A scale drawing shows an object or area scaled up or down so that it can be shown at a practical size. In a scale drawing, every measurement is scaled up or down by the same amount. In this drawing of the inventor's study, the scale is 1 cm : 1 m, which means that 1 cm in the drawing represents 1 m in real life. Do a scale drawing of a room in your house in the space below. Choose a scale factor that will allow it to fit the space.

The desk is 2 cm long in the drawing, which means it is 2 m long in real life.

SCALE 1 cm : 1 m

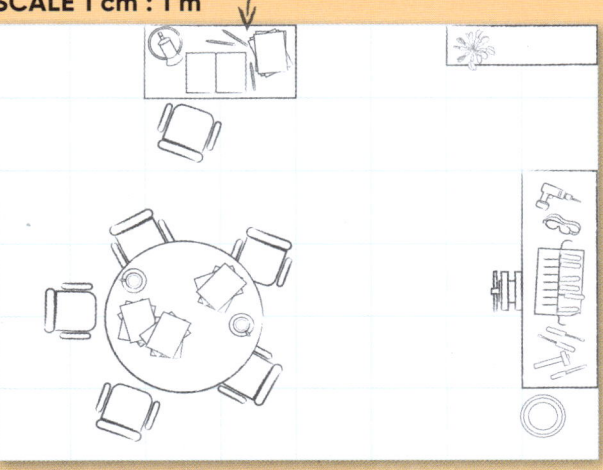

DRAW IT!

SCALE 1 cm : ....

DESIGN A ROCKET

Can you help the inventor design a rocket to travel into space? In the space below, draw a rocket to a scale of 1 cm : 1 m. Each square below is 1 cm. In real life, your rocket needs to be 16 m tall and 4 m wide at its widest point. It should have two windows that are each 2 m wide. The rest is up to you! Once you've finished, colour it in.

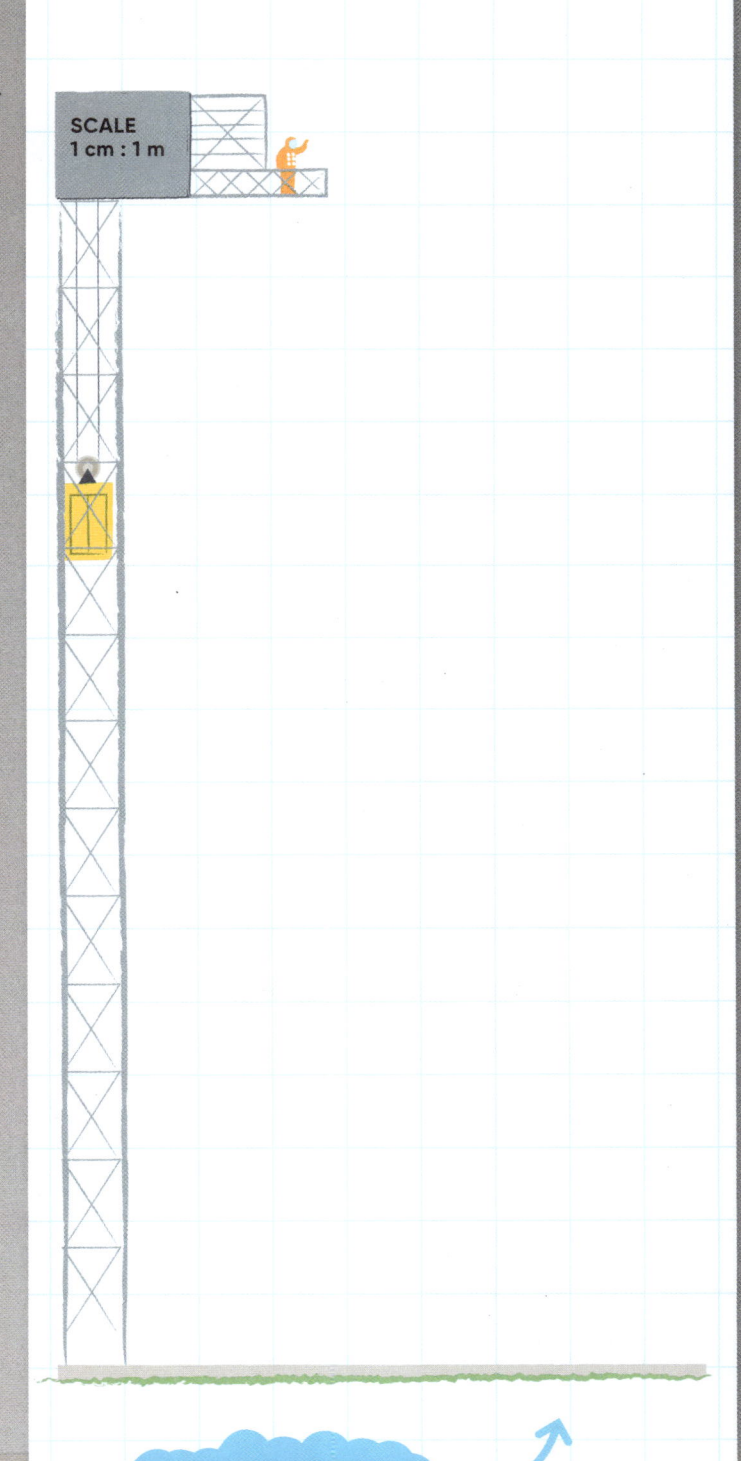

SCALE 1 cm : 1 m

DESIGN IT!

MEASURING

Measuring allows us to compare and record the sizes or amounts of things. In the UK, we use a system of measurement called the metric system, which uses units based on the number 10.

ANCIENT MEASUREMENTS (AND SOME MODERN ONES) WERE BASED ON SIZES OF HUMAN BODY PARTS, SUCH AS HANDS.

Units of measurement
We use different sets of units to measure different things. They come in lots of different sizes so you can accurately measure and record things that are very big or very small.

Volume
Volume is the amount of space something takes up. The volumes of liquids can be measured using millilitres (ml), and litres (l).

Weight
Weight is how heavy something is. It can be measured in milligrams (mg), grams (g), and kilograms (kg).

Temperature
Temperature tells us how hot or cold something is. Temperatures can be measured in degrees Celsius (°C).

Thermometers are used to measure temperature.

Measuring jugs can be used to measure volume.

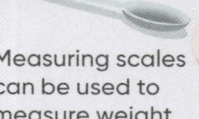

Measuring scales can be used to measure weight.

Length
The distance between two points is called length. Lengths can be measured in millimetres (mm), centimetres (cm), metres (m), and kilometres (km).

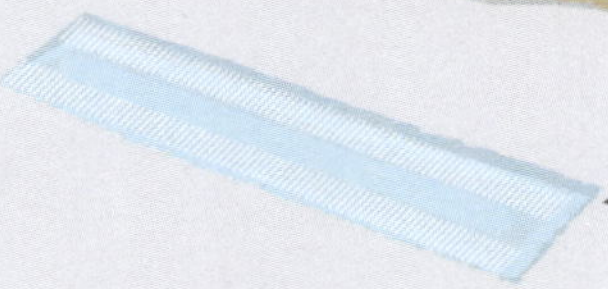

Rulers can be used to measure length.

WHICH UNIT?
Circle the unit that would be most appropriate for measuring each of these items. We've done the first one for you.

CIRCLE IT!

CAKE WIDTH	MILK VOLUME	FLOUR WEIGHT	WATER TEMPERATURE	BUTTER WEIGHT
(cm) / °C	ml / m	ml / kg	cm / °C	g / l

44

Converting units

When doing calculations with measurements, it's important to make sure the measurements are all in the same unit before you start. For units of weight, you multiply or divide a unit by 1,000 to convert it to the next, because there are 1,000 mg in 1 g, 1,000 g in 1 kg, and 1,000 kg in 1 tonne.

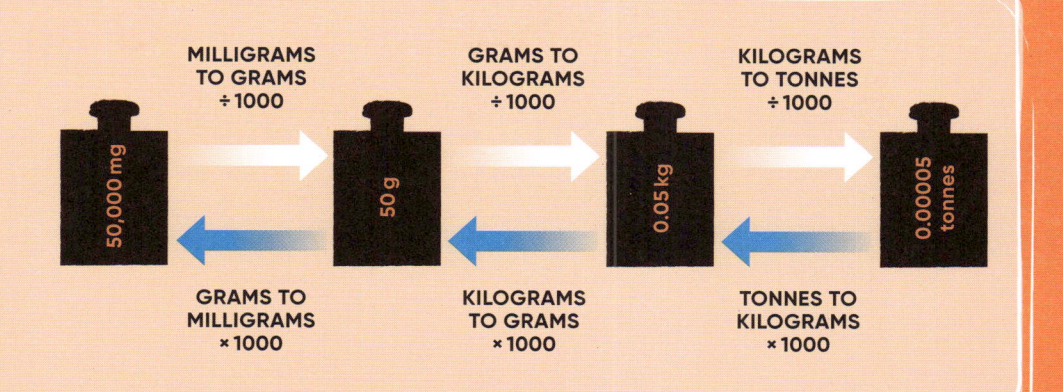

MILLIGRAMS TO GRAMS ÷ 1000 → GRAMS TO KILOGRAMS ÷ 1000 → KILOGRAMS TO TONNES ÷ 1000

50,000 mg → 50 g → 0.05 kg → 0.00005 tonnes

GRAMS TO MILLIGRAMS × 1000 ← KILOGRAMS TO GRAMS × 1000 ← TONNES TO KILOGRAMS × 1000

HOW HEAVY?

How much does the curry in this saucepan weigh in **kilograms** in total? Use the spaces below to add together the weight of the ingredients. You'll need to convert the measurements that are given in grams to kilograms before you add them all together.

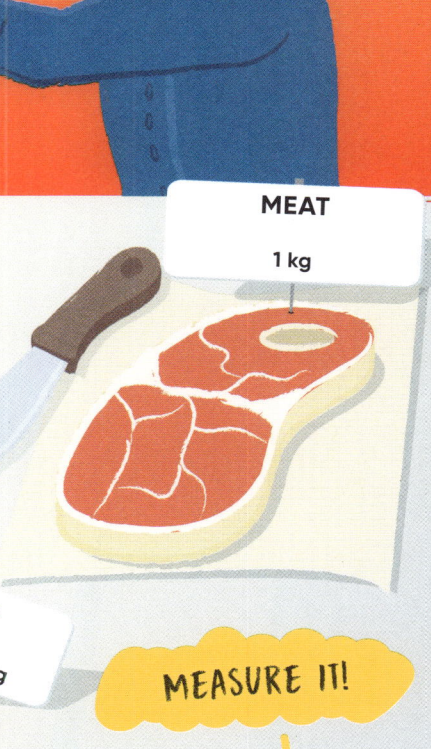

ONION
200 g = ... kg

SPICES
100 g = ... kg

POTATO
500 g = ... kg

TOMATO
400 g = ... kg

MEAT
1 kg

MEASURE IT!

____ kg + ____ kg + ____ kg + ____ kg + ____ kg = ____ kg
ONION   SPICES   POTATO   TOMATO   MEAT   TOTAL

PERIMETER

The distance around the outside edge of a closed two-dimensional shape is called its perimeter. It's the length of the path that goes around the edges of a whole shape. For example, a triangle's perimeter is the total length of its three sides.

BONUS QUESTION
Which one of your books has the largest perimeter? Use a ruler or tape measure to find the lengths of the four sides, then add them together.

Finding the perimeter
To find a shape's perimeter, we simply add together the lengths of all its sides. It works the same way no matter what the shape is, from a simple rectangle to a more complicated shape.

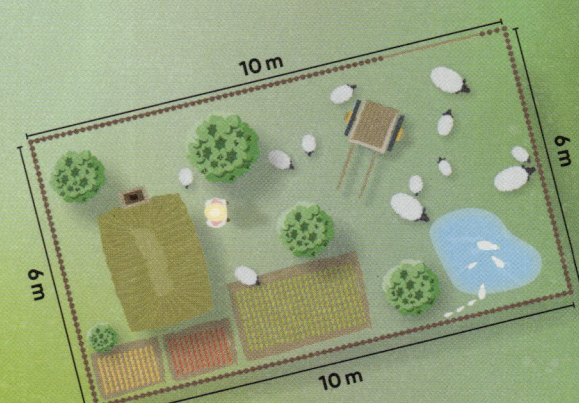

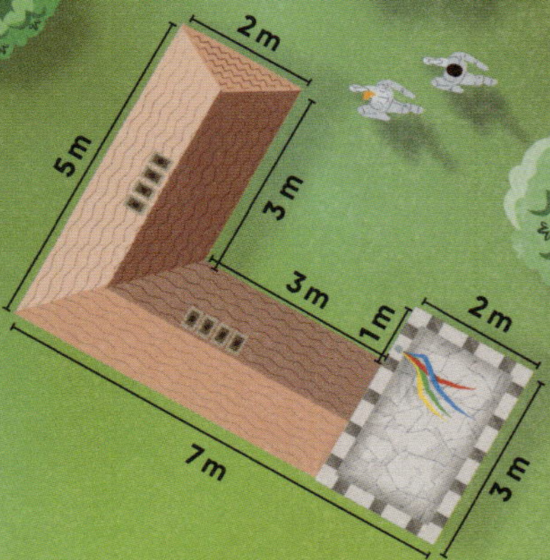

PERIMETER =
6 + 10 + 6 + 10 = 32 m

PERIMETER =
5 + 2 + 3 + 3 + 1 + 2 + 3 + 7 = 26 m

MATCH THE MEASUREMENTS
Find the perimeter for each of these shapes, then draw lines to match each one to its perimeter measurement. We've done one for you.

MATCH IT!

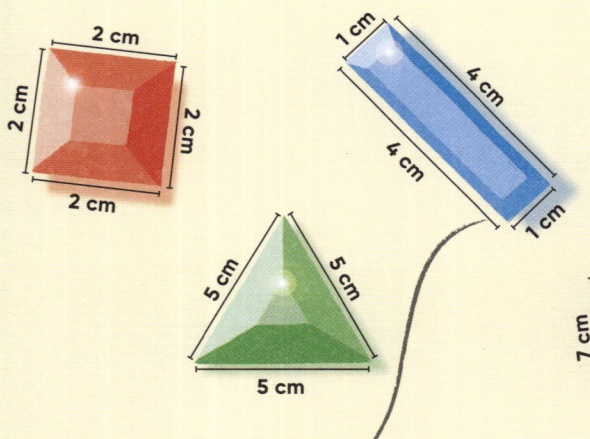

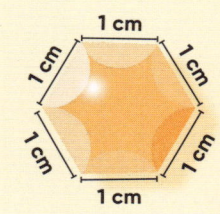

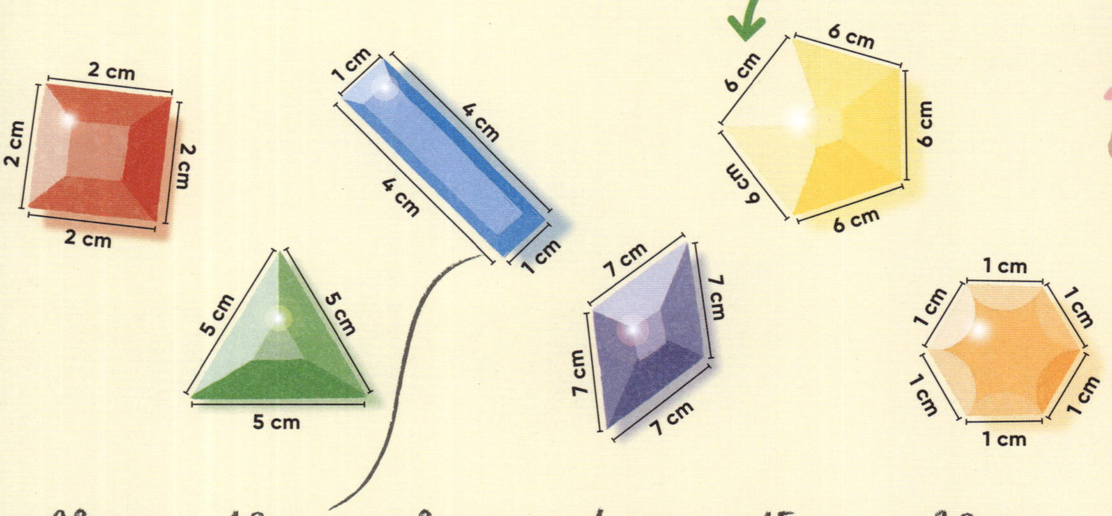

28 cm   10 cm   8 cm   6 cm   15 cm   30 cm

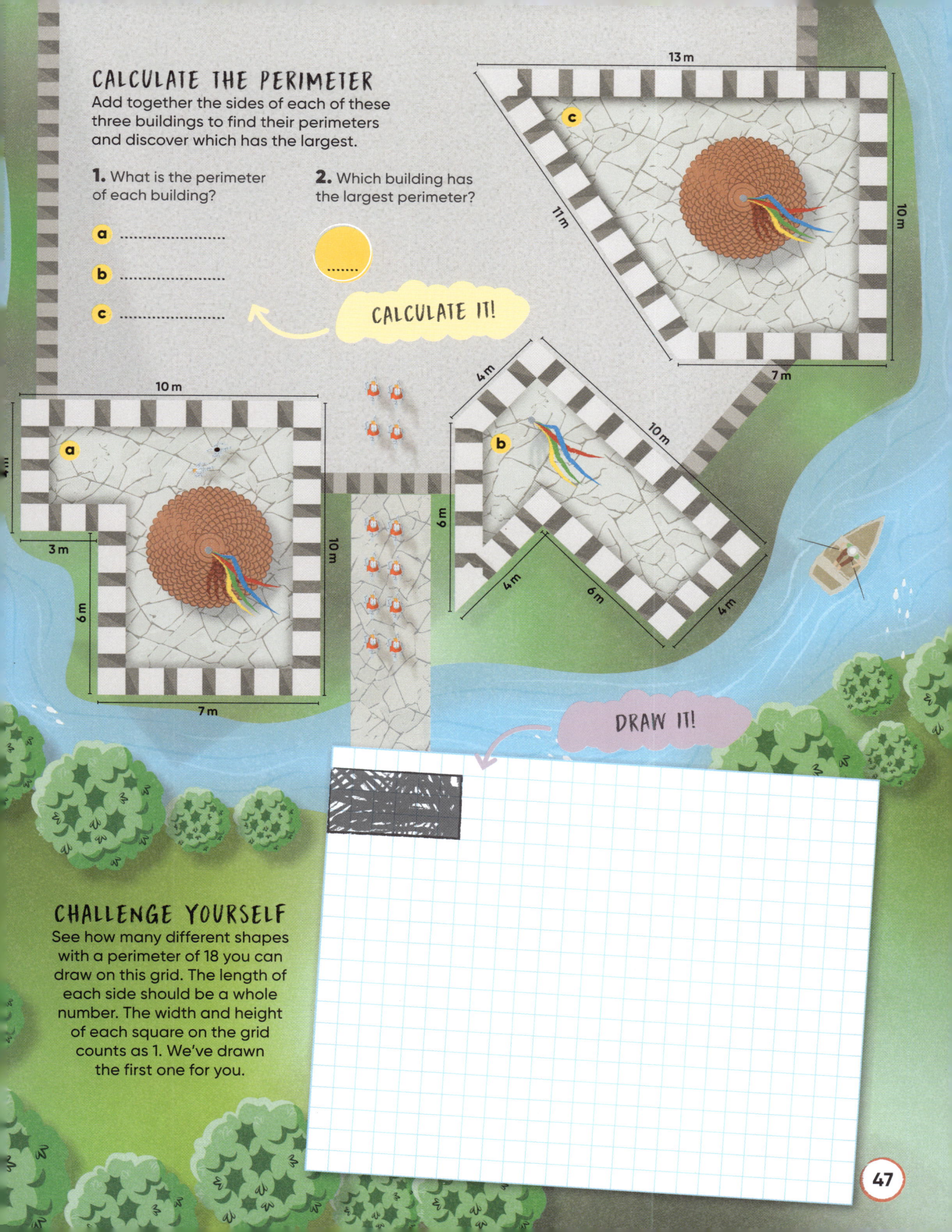

CALCULATE THE PERIMETER

Add together the sides of each of these three buildings to find their perimeters and discover which has the largest.

1. What is the perimeter of each building?

a ....

b ....

c ....

2. Which building has the largest perimeter?

....

CALCULATE IT!

DRAW IT!

CHALLENGE YOURSELF

See how many different shapes with a perimeter of 18 you can draw on this grid. The length of each side should be a whole number. The width and height of each square on the grid counts as 1. We've drawn the first one for you.

47

AREA

The total space inside a closed, two-dimensional shape is known as its area. Area is measured using units called squared units, such as **cm²** and **m²**. They are based on the units we use to measure length. We can calculate a shape's area by counting the square units that make it up or by using a handy formula.

Counting squares

We can find the area of a shape by counting the number of squared units it contains. This rectangle is made up of eight 1 m² squares, so the total area of the rectangle is 8 m².

$1 + 1 + 1 + 1 + 1 + 1 + 1 + 1 = 8$

Each square is 1 m².

COUNT THE SQUARES

Find the areas of the playgrounds below by counting their square metres. Which one has the largest area and which one has the smallest area?

FIND IT!

..... LARGEST PLAYGROUND

..... SMALLEST PLAYGROUND

a .... m²

b .... m²

Each square is 1 m².

c .... m²

d .... m²

ESTIMATE THE AREA

We can use square grids to estimate (roughly work out) the area of unusual shapes. Full squares count as 1, and part squares count as half. So, to find the area, we divide the number of part squares by 2 and add that to the number of full squares. Try estimating the areas of these ponds.

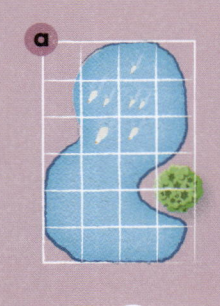

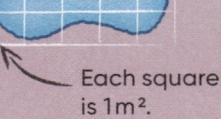

ESTIMATE IT!

Each square is 1 m².

	a	b	c	d
FULL SQUARES	10			
PART SQUARES	14			
TOTAL AREA	$10 + (14 \div 2) = 17 m^2$			

A formula for area

In maths, we can use rules or relationships to help us do calculations more quickly or easily. These rules are called formulas. The formula for the area of a square or rectangle is:

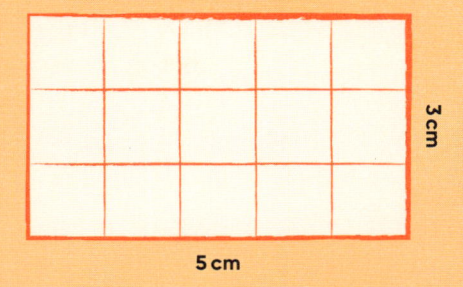

AREA = LENGTH × WIDTH

$5 \times 3 = 15 \text{ cm}^2$

USE THE FORMULA

Use the formula for area to find the area of these squares and rectangles.

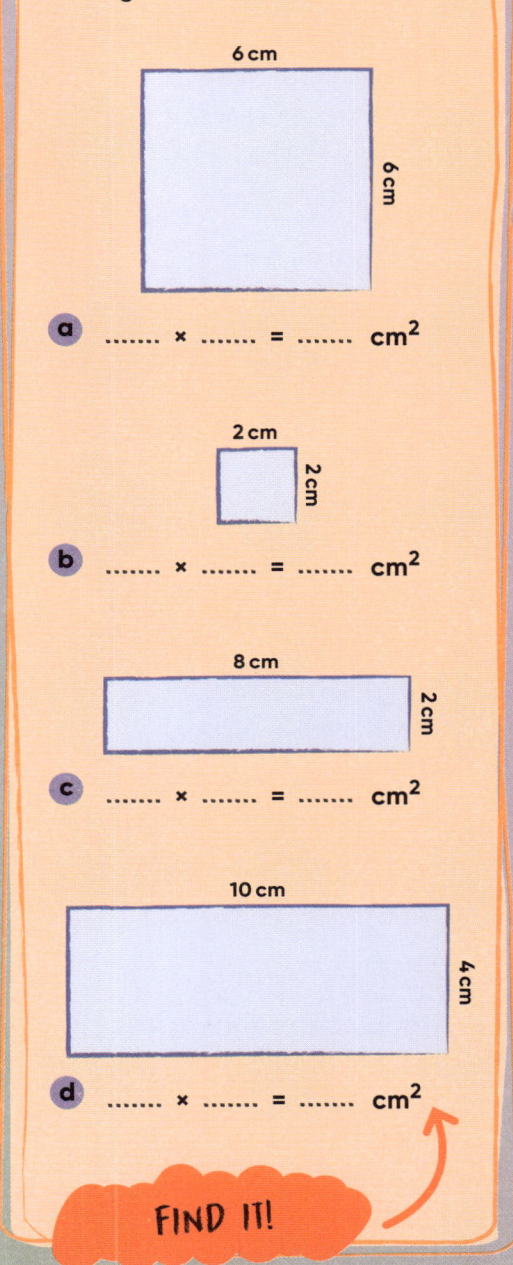

6 cm × 6 cm

a .... × .... = ... cm²

2 cm × 2 cm

b .... × .... = ... cm²

8 cm × 2 cm

c .... × .... = ... cm²

10 cm × 4 cm

d .... × .... = ... cm²

FIND IT!

WHICH RECTANGLES?

This grid has been divided up into lots of rectangles. Colour in all the rectangles that have an area of 12 cm².

COLOUR IT!

BONUS QUESTION

Find a piece of squared paper and see how many different shapes you can draw with an area of 24 cm².

VOLUME

The volume of a three-dimensional shape is the total amount of space it takes up. The units we use to measure volume are based on the units we use to measure length. Volume is measured in units called cubed units, such as **cm³** and **m³**.

Counting cubes
One way to find the volume of a shape is to count the number of cubed units it contains. This cuboid has a volume of 96 m³ because it is made up of 96 cubes that are each 1 m³ in volume.

VOLUME AND CAPACITY
While volume is a measure of the space a 3-D shape takes up, capacity is a measure of the space inside a shape or the amount it can hold.

Each cube is 1 m³

COUNT THE CUBES
Find the volume of each of these three-dimensional shapes by counting the square cubes, then draw lines to match each one to the correct volume. Each cube represents 1 m³.

MATCH IT!

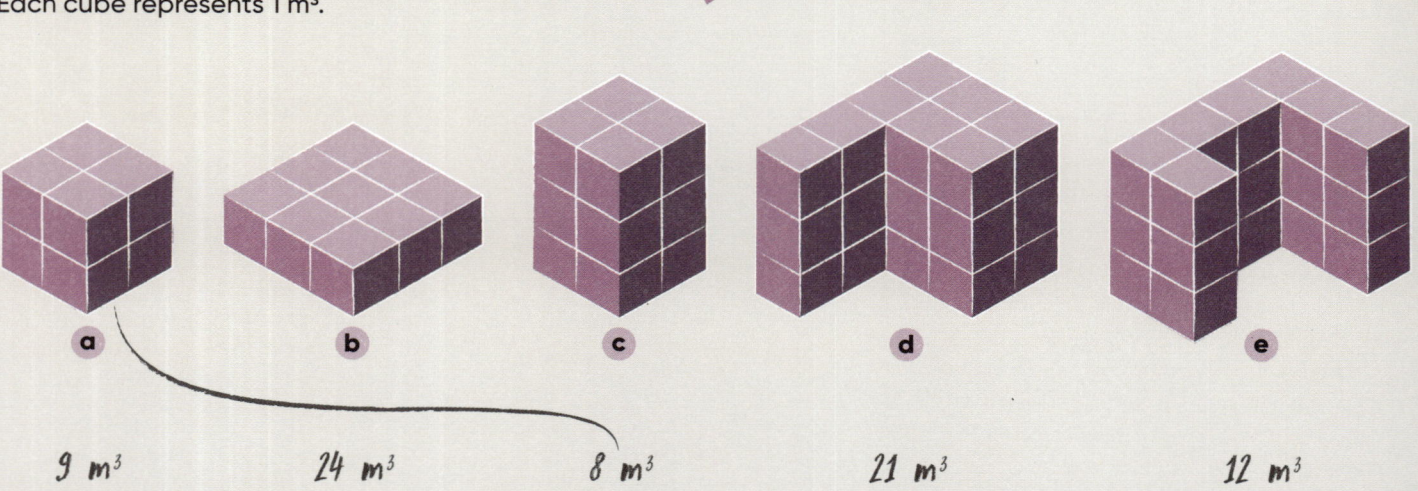

a   b   c   d   e

9 m³   24 m³   8 m³   21 m³   12 m³

50

A formula for volume

It can be very time-consuming to count all the cubes in a 3-D shape, so sometimes it's simpler to use a formula. The formula for the volume of a cube or cuboid is:

VOLUME = LENGTH × WIDTH × HEIGHT

$5 \times 2 \times 4 = 40 \, m^3$

CALCULATE THE VOLUME

Use the formula for volume to calculate the volume of each of these cubes and cuboids in m^3.

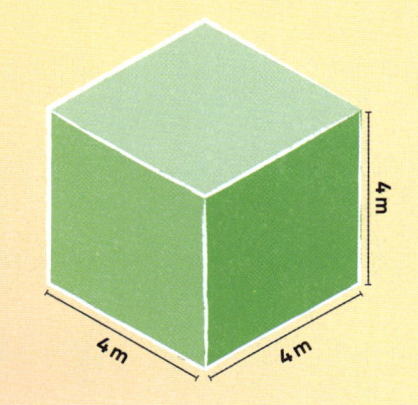

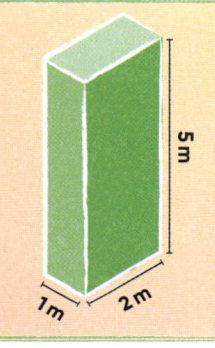

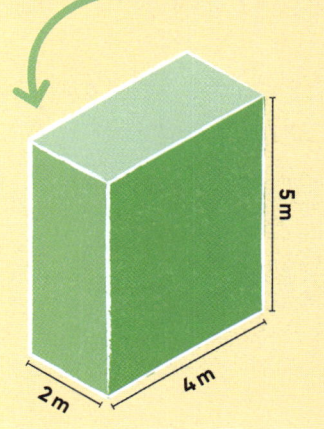

WORK IT OUT!

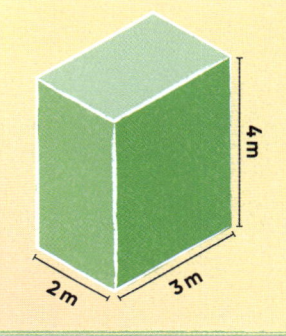

a) ...... × ...... × ...... = ... m^3

b) ...... × ...... × ...... = ... m^3

c) ...... × ...... × ...... = ... m^3

d) ...... × ...... × ...... = ... m^3

ORDER BY VOLUME

Number these shapes in order of size. Use 5 for the shape with the largest volume, and 1 for the shape with the smallest volume.

ORDER IT!

TIME

Being able to keep track of the passing of time each day by using seconds, minutes, and hours helps us to organize our lives. There are 24 hours in a day, 60 minutes in an hour, and 60 seconds in a minute.

THE FIRST CLOCKS WERE SUNDIALS USED BY **ANCIENT EGYPTIANS** AROUND 1500 BCE TO TRACK TIME USING THE SUN AND **SHADOWS**.

FILL IN THE TIME

Leo has a busy day ahead! Help him avoid being late for any of his activities by drawing minute hands onto the clocks below so they show the time that is written beneath them.

DRAW IT!

SEVEN O'CLOCK

HALF PAST ELEVEN

QUARTER PAST ONE

QUARTER TO FOUR

TEN TO NINE

TWENTY-FIVE PAST SIX

Reading time

We can use clocks to tell the time. The numbers show the hours and 60 small marks around the edge show the minutes. The long hand points to the minutes; the short hand indicates the hour. Together, they tell us the exact hour and minute.

HERE, THE TIME IS ONE O'CLOCK — When the minute hand points to 12, it is on the hour and we say it is "o'clock".

QUARTER PAST ONE — When the minute hand points to 3, the time is quarter past the hour.

TWENTY-THREE MINUTES PAST ONE — Before the minute hand reaches 6, we look at how many minutes have passed since the hour.

HALF PAST ONE — When the minute hand points to 6, the time is half past the hour.

QUARTER TO TWO — When the minute hand points to 9, the time is quarter to the next hour.

EIGHTEEN MINUTES TO TWO — When the minute hand passes 6, we look at how many minutes are left until the next hour.

MAKE IT DIGITAL

Digital clocks use just numbers and no hands to show the time. They often count 24 hours of the day, instead of 12 for the morning and 12 for the afternoon. For example, 13:00 means 1 pm and 14:00 means 2 pm. Draw lines to match these digital clocks to the clocks below that show the same time.

Minutes
Hours

18:10   3:00 pm   16:30   8:45 am   12:40

MATCH IT!

a   b   c   d   e

HOW LONG WILL IT TAKE?

Sometimes it can be helpful to convert times from one unit to another to make it easier to work with them. Can you work out how many minutes it takes this child to get home from school? Start by converting each period of time into minutes, then add the numbers together.

WRITE IT!

TIP!
To change seconds to minutes, divide the number by 60.
To convert hours to minutes, multiply the number by 60.

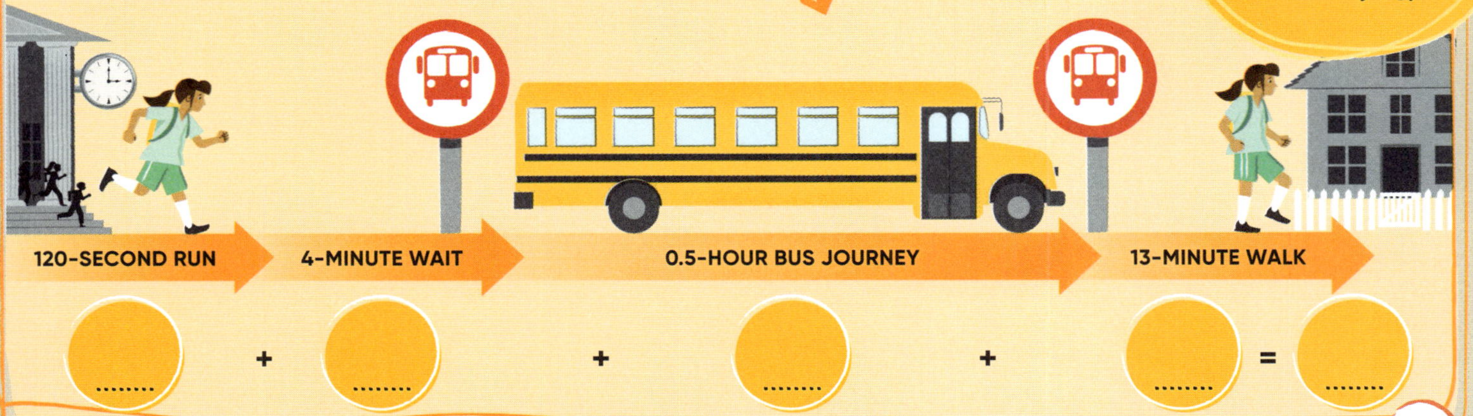

120-SECOND RUN   4-MINUTE WAIT   0.5-HOUR BUS JOURNEY   13-MINUTE WALK

.... + ... + ... + ... = ...

MONEY

Money is a unit of measurement that shows what things cost and can be exchanged to buy things. A system of money is called a currency. Today, most currencies are made up of coins and notes of various values. The UK currency uses pounds and pence – there are 100 pence in one pound.

Writing money
We write a "£" sign before an amount in pounds, or a "p" after an amount in pence. If an amount is a combination of the two, we write it as a decimal, with pounds to the left of the decimal place and pence to the right.

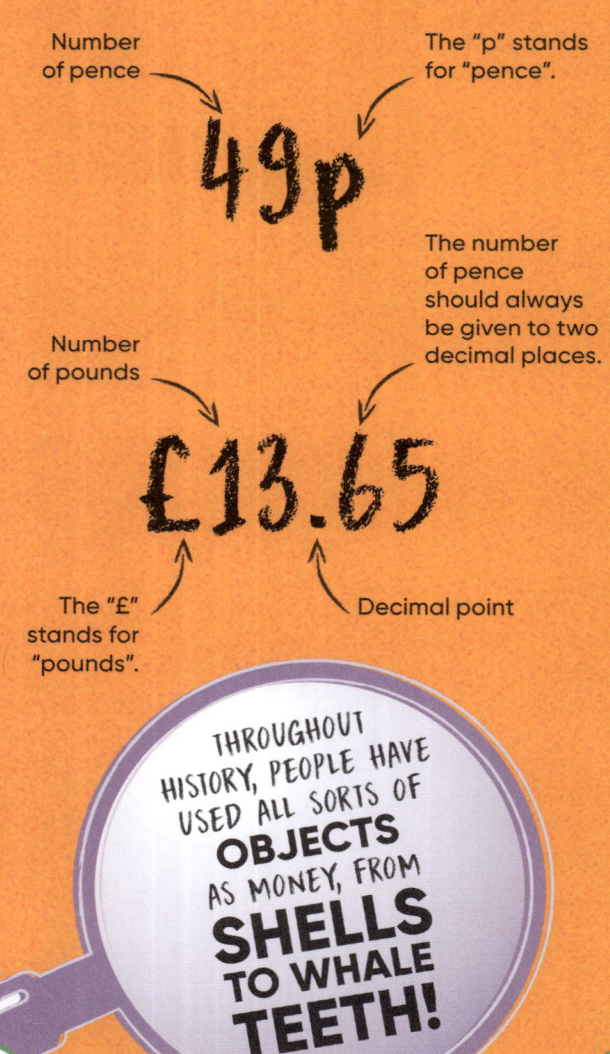

Number of pence → **49p** ← The "p" stands for "pence".

The number of pence should always be given to two decimal places.

Number of pounds → **£13.65** ← Decimal point

The "£" stands for "pounds".

THROUGHOUT HISTORY, PEOPLE HAVE USED ALL SORTS OF **OBJECTS** AS MONEY, FROM **SHELLS** TO WHALE **TEETH!**

MATCH THE MONEY
Draw lines to match each of these fancy-dress outfits with the exact money you would need to buy it. We've done the first one for you.

MATCH IT!

- £15.50 (superhero)
- 37p (glasses and moustache)
- £4.40 (wizard hat and beard)
- 65p (pirate hat)
- £32.70 (dinosaur)

a £2, £1, £1, 20p, 20p

b £10, £5, 50p

c 20p, 10p, 5p, 2p

d £20, £2, 50p, £10, 20p

e 50p, 10p, 5p

WHAT'S THE CHANGE?

How much change would you be given if you paid for each of these baskets of shopping using a £20 note? To work it out, simply subtract the cost of the basket from £20, as in the first example we've done for you.

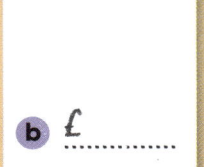

WRITE IT!

Baskets: £18, £6.50, 50p, £14, £9.50

20 − 18 = 2

a. £ 2
b. £ ......
c. £ ......
d. £ ......
e. £ ......

GET DRESSED UP!

Pick out a fancy-dress outfit from the items below and draw the outfit you choose in the mirror. Work out how much the outfit will cost and write the total in the box. Use a calculator to check your answer.

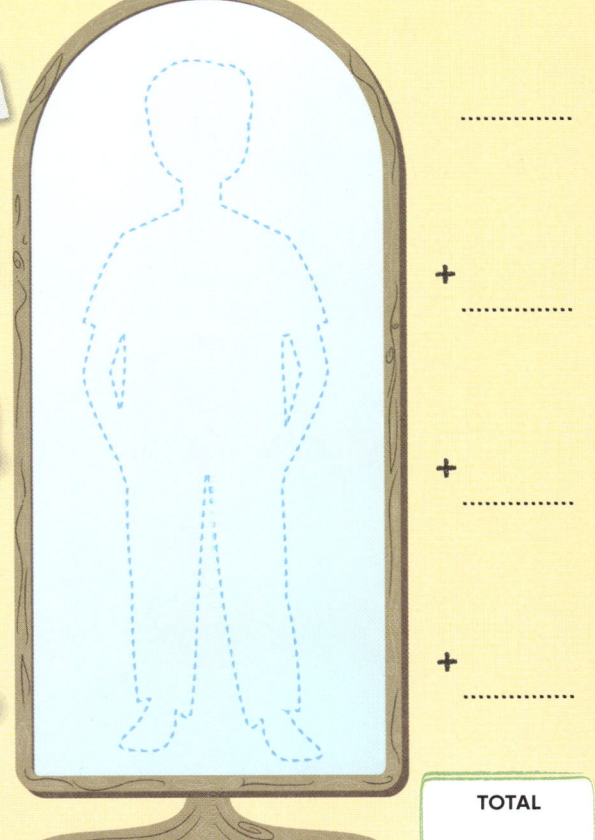

ADD IT!

Items:
- Crown £1.33
- Clown wig/hat £1.05
- Astronaut helmet 99p
- Colourful jacket £5.22
- Shirt £3.99
- Vest £2.45
- White trousers £5
- Pink trousers with belt £6.33
- Striped trousers £7.12
- Pointy shoes £1.75
- Sneakers £2.18
- White boots £1.99

......
+ ......
+ ......
+ ......

TOTAL
£ ......

LINES

Lines join two points together. In maths, they are thought of as one-dimensional – they have length but no thickness. Lines can be straight or curved, and a straight line always shows the shortest possible distance between two points.

HOW MANY DIMENSIONS?
Lines have length but no width, so they are one-dimensional. Shapes are only two-dimensional if they have both length and width.

WHICH LINE?
Can you spot all the different types of lines in this crane? Colour the horizontal lines in red, the vertical lines in blue, and the diagonal lines in green. Draw right-angle marks where perpendicular lines meet, then find three pairs of parallel lines and draw arrowheads to mark them.

Colouring key
- Horizontal lines
- Vertical lines
- Diagonal lines

COLOUR IT!

FINISH THE HOUSE
Four of the perpendicular lines are missing from the windows of this house. Can you help the builders complete the building by drawing in the missing lines with a ruler? We've drawn the first one for you.

DRAW IT!

Types of lines

Lines can be named according to their direction or how they are positioned compared to other lines.

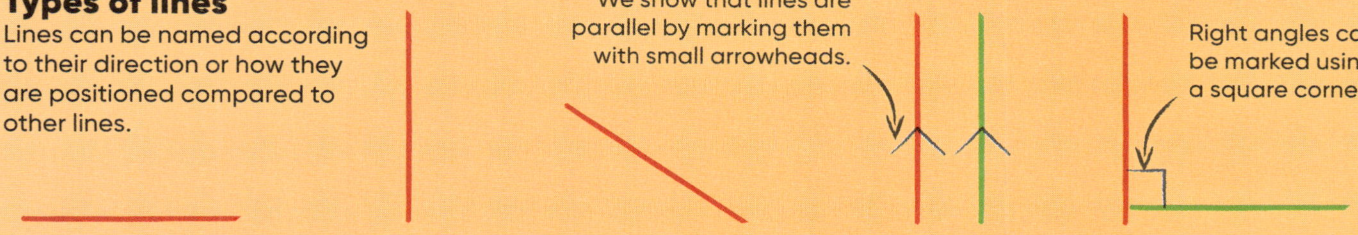

Horizontal
A horizontal line is a level line that goes from side to side.

Vertical
A vertical line goes straight up and down.

Diagonal
A diagonal line is slanted – it is straight but not horizontal or vertical.

We show that lines are parallel by marking them with small arrowheads.

Parallel
Lines are parallel to each other if they are the same distance apart all along, and never meet.

Right angles can be marked using a square corner.

Perpendicular
Two lines are described as perpendicular when they are at right angles (90°) to each other.

FIND THE LINES

Can you find the names of the different types of lines in the word search below? Hint: one answer goes round a corner and another appears twice.

Diagonal
Horizontal
Perpendicular
Vertical
Parallel

F	G	W	R	T	U	Q	E	R	T	Y	O
S	D	F	G	H	J	D	L	W	R	H	J
A	V	D	P	G	E	R	T	K	G	P	E
P	E	R	P	E	N	H	B	F	Z	X	Q
Y	R	J	M	D	D	T	G	V	C	S	W
B	T	H	O	R	I	Z	O	N	T	A	L
O	I	Y	G	E	C	A	K	D	M	K	Z
U	C	J	B	V	U	H	G	S	L	X	B
P	A	R	A	L	L	E	L	O	H	O	F
X	L	E	L	L	A	R	A	P	N	W	N
N	P	V	E	J	R	A	D	E	Z	A	E
Q	Z	I	M	O	A	W	X	C	H	S	L
L	A	F	B	I	B	A	G	L	R	I	K

FIND IT!

DESIGN A SKYSCRAPER

The mayor of Linington has asked you to design a new skyscraper for the city. She would like it to include plenty of different types of lines. Use this space to design your skyscraper, then colour it in.

DRAW IT!

57

ANGLES

An angle is made when two lines meet at a shared point. The amount of turn between the two lines is measured in units called degrees. Degrees are written using the symbol °.

Measuring angles
You can use a transparent tool called a protractor to measure the size of an angle. First, place the protractor so its centre sits directly over the point of the angle, with one side of the angle lined up with 0, then read where the other side of the angle meets the scale.

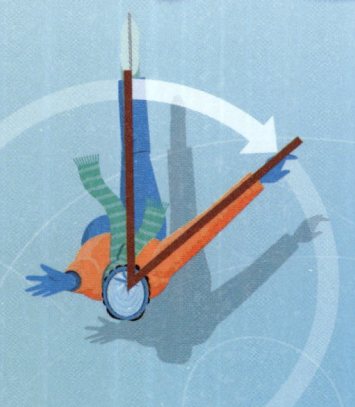

Types of angles
Angles are grouped into six different types, depending on their size. They are each based on their proportion of one full turn, or circle.

Acute angle
An angle that measures between 0° and 90° is called an acute angle.

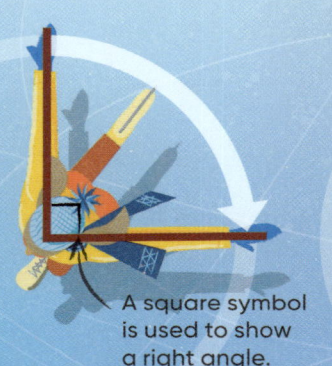

Right angle
An angle that measures exactly 90° is called a right angle or quarter turn.

A square symbol is used to show a right angle.

Obtuse angle
An angle that measures between 90° and 180° is called an obtuse angle.

NAME THE ANGLES
Use the information above to help you fill in which type of angle is shown in each of these examples. We've done the first one for you.

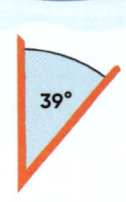

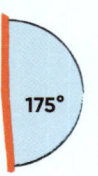

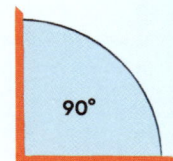

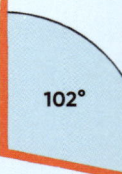

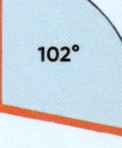

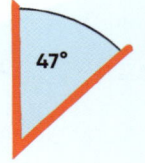

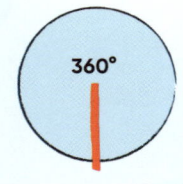

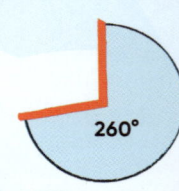

NAME IT!

a) 39° — Acute angle
b) 175° ....
c) 90° ....
d) 102° ....
e) 47° ....
f) 180° ....
g) 360° ....
h) 260° ....

FIND THE ANGLES IN YOUR NAME

Angles are everywhere, even in the letters in your name. Write your name here in capital letters with straight lines, then use a protractor to measure the sizes of the angles in each letter.

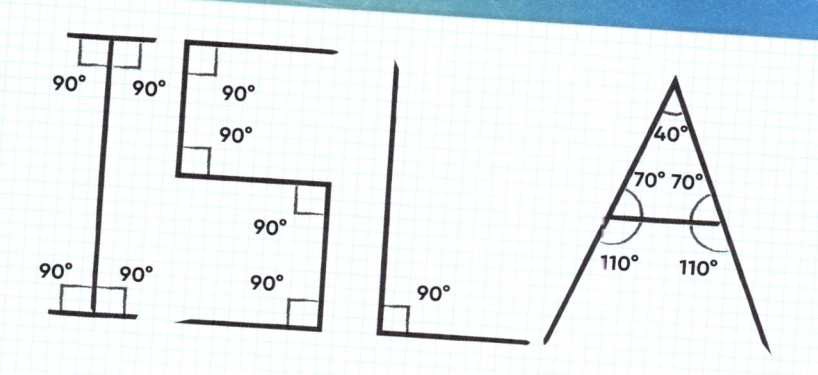

WRITE IT!

ISLA
(90°, 90°, 90°, 90°, 90°, 90°, 90°, 90°, 90°, 40°, 70°, 70°, 110°, 110°)

Half turn
An angle that measures exactly 180° is a straight line and is called a half turn.

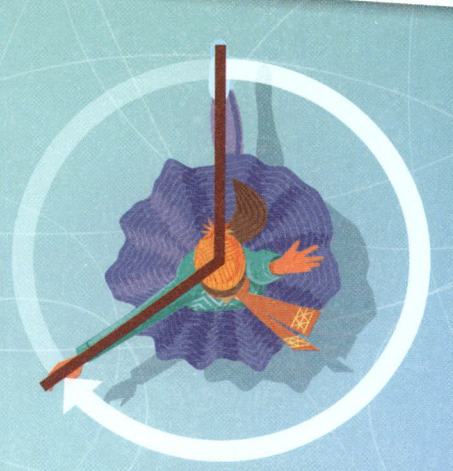

Reflex angle
An angle that measures between 180° and 360° is called a reflex angle.

Full turn
An angle of 360° is known as a full turn because there are 360° in a circle.

HOW BIG?

Knowing the size of full, half, and quarter turn angles can help you to work out the sizes of unknown angles within them. Angles in a right angle always add up to 90°, angles on a straight line or half turn add up to 180°, and angles in a full turn add up to 360°. Can you work out the sizes of these missing angles? We've done one for you.

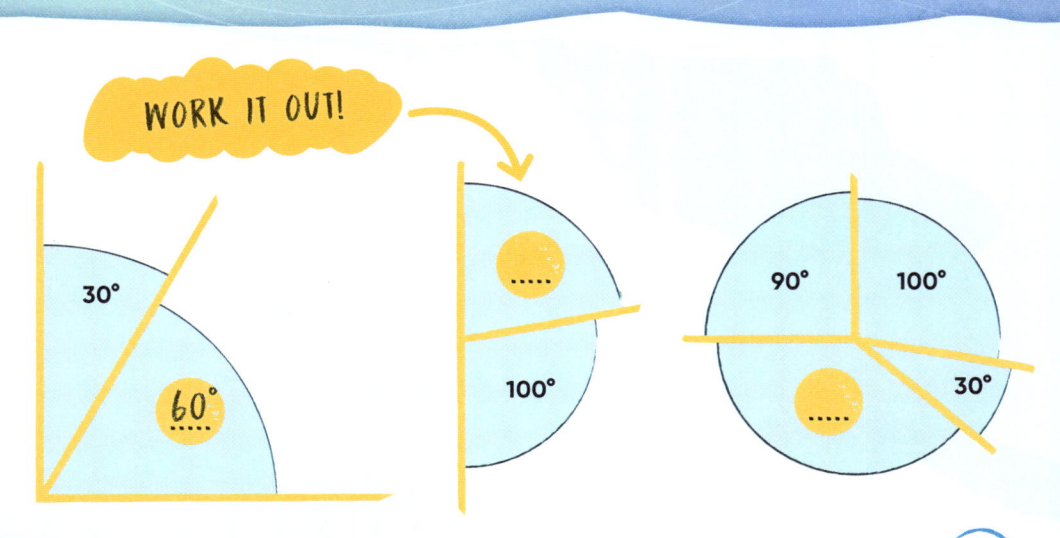

WORK IT OUT!

30°, 60°

....., 100°

90°, 100°, 30°, ...

59

TRIANGLES

A triangle is a shape with three sides and three internal angles that always add up to 180°. The points where sides meet are called vertices. The topmost vertex opposite the triangle's base is called the apex.

Types of triangles

Triangles have different names, depending on the sizes of their angles and the lengths of their sides. On these diagrams, dashes show sides that have equal lengths. Right angles are marked with squares and equal angles with arcs.

Dashes mark sides of equal length.

Equilateral triangle
A triangle with sides that are all equal in length and angles that are all equal in size (60°) is called an equilateral triangle.

Arcs mark equal angles.

Isosceles triangle
An isosceles triangle has two sides that are the same length. The two angles opposite the equal sides are also equal.

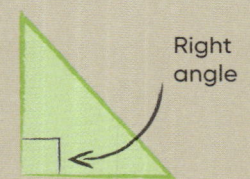

Right angle

Right-angled triangle
A right-angled triangle is named for the 90° angle where two of the sides meet. A 90° angle is called a right angle.

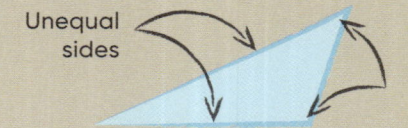

Unequal sides *Unequal angles*

Scalene triangle
A scalene triangle is a triangle with sides that are all different lengths, and angles that are all different sizes.

ALL HANDS ON DECK!

There are triangles as far as the eye can see in this harbour. Colour in all the white triangles you can see using the colours below. Count up how many of each type of triangle you found and write the numbers in the spaces below.

Colouring key

〜 Equilateral triangles   .....

〜 Isosceles triangles   .....

〜 Right-angled triangles   .....

〜 Scalene triangles   .....

Total number of triangles   .....

COUNT IT!

BONUS QUESTION

From blocks of cheese to clothes hangers, triangles can be found all over your home. How many can you find?

....

QUADRILATERALS

Flat shapes with four sides are called quadrilaterals. Every quadrilateral is made up of four sides, four internal angles, and four corners (called vertices).

ONLY TWO QUADRILATERALS HAVE SIDES THAT ARE ALL THE SAME LENGTH: THE SQUARE AND THE RHOMBUS.

Types of quadrilaterals

There are seven different types of quadrilateral. On these diagrams, matching pairs of arrows on opposite sides show they are parallel, and matching dashes show that sides are equal in length. Right angles are marked with square corners, and equal angles are shown with arcs.

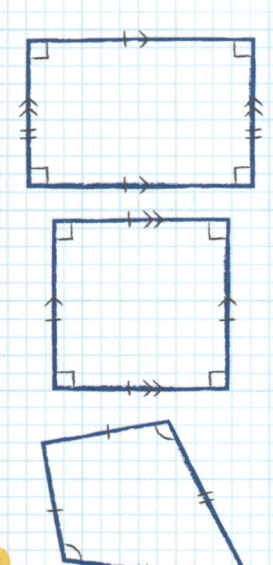

Rectangle
A rectangle has two pairs of parallel sides, and the sides in each pair are equal in length. All four angles are right angles.

Square
A square is a type of rectangle with two pairs of parallel sides that are all equal in length. Its four angles are all right angles.

Kite
A kite has two pairs of equal sides that are adjacent (next to) each other, rather than opposite. A kite also has one set of equal opposite angles.

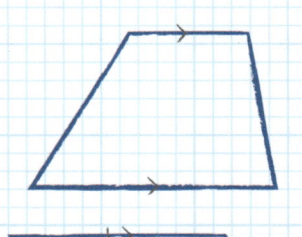

Trapezium
A trapezium has one pair of parallel sides that are not equal in length. Its other set of sides may be equal or unequal.

Parallelogram
A parallelogram has two pairs of parallel sides. Its pairs of opposite angles and opposite sides are always equal in size.

Rhombus
A rhombus is like a slanted square, with pairs of parallel sides that are all the same length. Its opposite angles are equal, but not right angles.

Irregular quadrilateral
An irregular quadrilateral has no parallel sides and no equal angles. All four of its sides are different lengths.

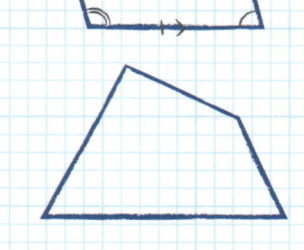

CREATE QUADRILATERAL ART

Some shapes can fit together without any gaps. This is called tessellation. Identical quadrilaterals will always tessellate. Finish the tessellations below by copying the quadrilateral used in each one.

DRAW IT!

FINISH THE FLOWCHART

Use what you have learnt to help you complete this flowchart. Use the questions to help you work out which quadrilateral belongs in each space below, then write their names and draw them in the correct spaces. We've done the first one for you.

START!

Are all four interior angles right angles?

- Yes → Are all four sides the same length?
  - Yes → **a. Square**
  - No → **d. ....**
- No → Are there two pairs of equal opposite angles?
  - Yes → Are all four sides the same length?
    - Yes → **b. ....**
    - No → **e. ....**
  - No → Are any pairs of sides parallel?
    - Yes → **g. ....**
    - No → Are any adjacent sides the same length?
      - Yes → **c. ....**
      - No → **f. ....**

COMPLETE IT!

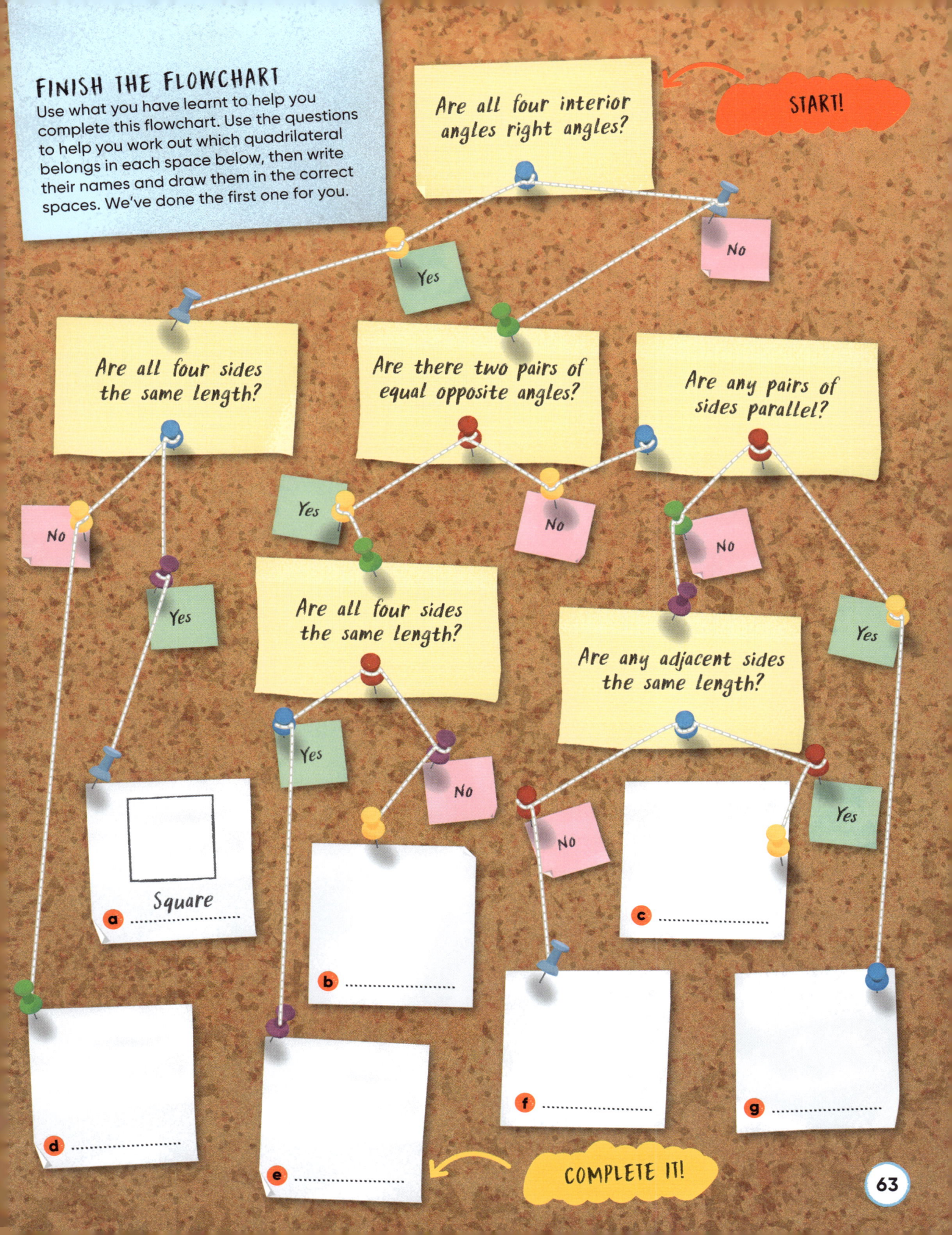

63

Regular polygons

Polygons with sides that are all the same length are called regular polygons. Here are some examples. Use a pencil to trace the edges of each one. We've done the first one for you.

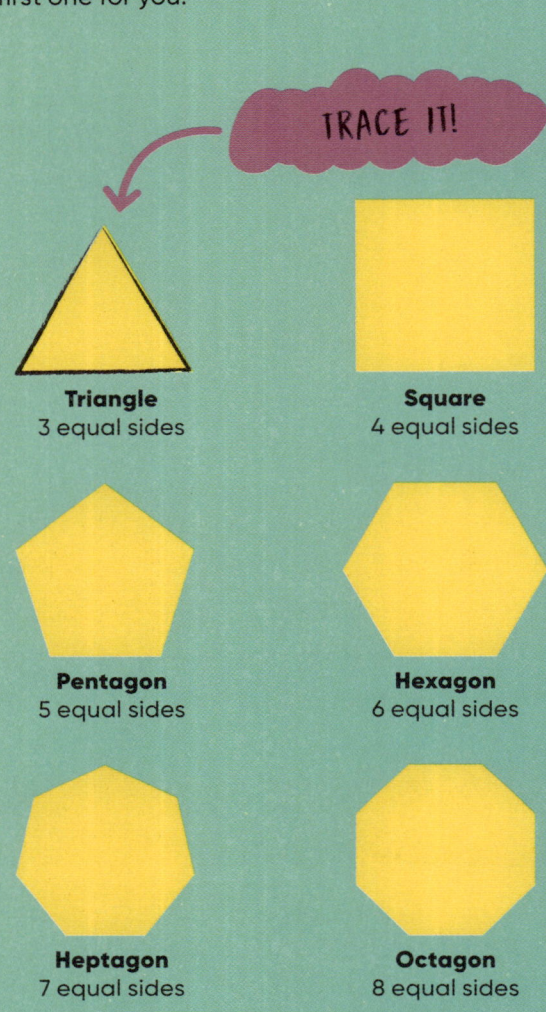

TRACE IT!

Triangle
3 equal sides

Square
4 equal sides

Pentagon
5 equal sides

Hexagon
6 equal sides

Heptagon
7 equal sides

Octagon
8 equal sides

Nonagon
9 equal sides

Decagon
10 equal sides

Hendecagon
11 equal sides

Dodecagon
12 equal sides

POLYGONS

Polygons are flat shapes that have three or more straight sides. They are two-dimensional (2-D), which means they have height and length, but no thickness or depth.

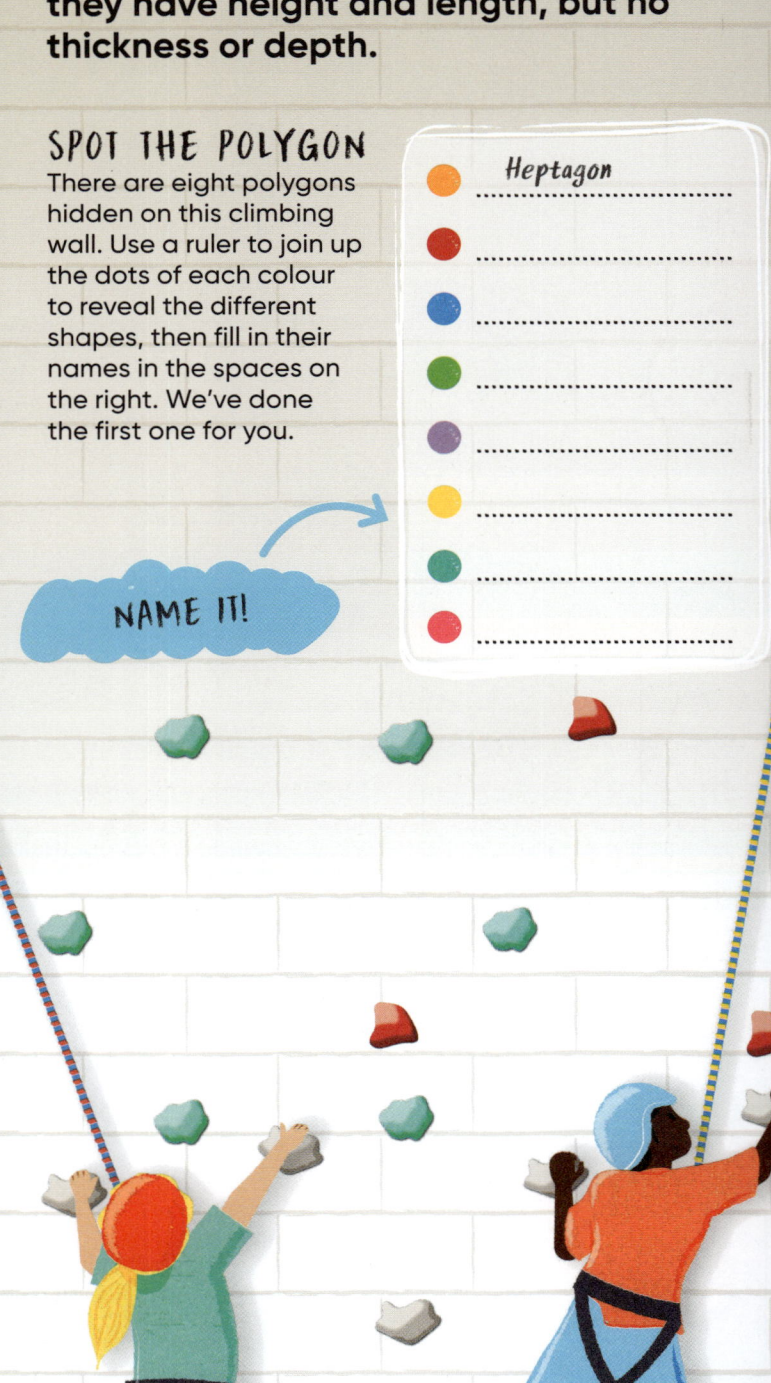

SPOT THE POLYGON

There are eight polygons hidden on this climbing wall. Use a ruler to join up the dots of each colour to reveal the different shapes, then fill in their names in the spaces on the right. We've done the first one for you.

NAME IT!

- Heptagon
- ....
- ....
- ....
- ....
- ....
- ....
- ....

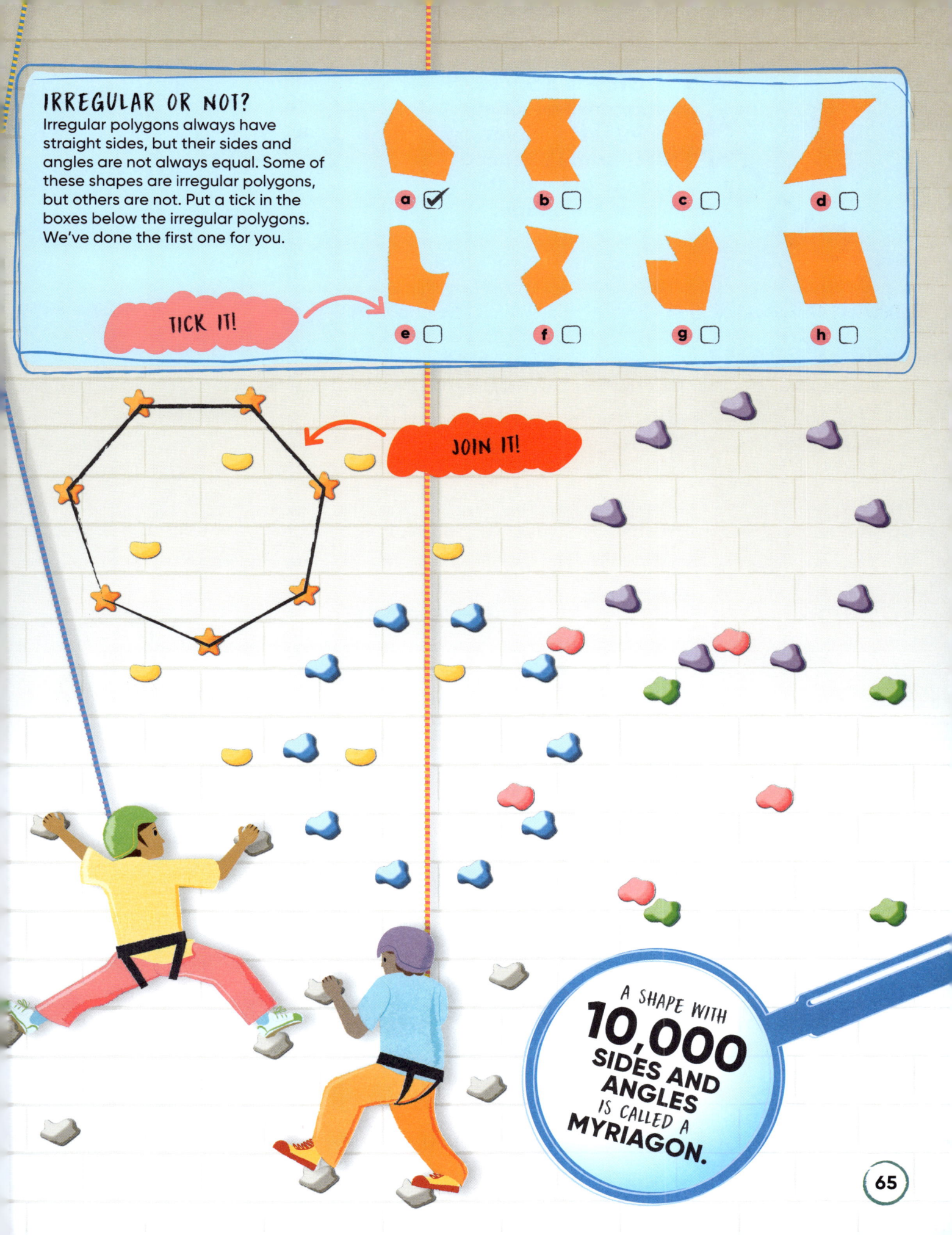

IRREGULAR OR NOT?

Irregular polygons always have straight sides, but their sides and angles are not always equal. Some of these shapes are irregular polygons, but others are not. Put a tick in the boxes below the irregular polygons. We've done the first one for you.

a ✓   b ☐   c ☐   d ☐

e ☐   f ☐   g ☐   h ☐

TICK IT!

JOIN IT!

A SHAPE WITH **10,000** SIDES AND ANGLES IS CALLED A **MYRIAGON.**

CIRCLES

A circle is a round shape where every point on its boundary is the same distance from the point at the centre of the shape.

THE ANCIENT **EGYPTIANS** WERE AMONG THE FIRST PEOPLE TO STUDY CIRCLES IN DETAIL, **THOUSANDS OF YEARS AGO.**

Parts of a circle

Circles can be divided up and measured in ways that most other shapes cannot. Here are the names of the different parts of a circle.

Segment
The smaller of the two parts of a circle created when it is divided by a chord

Circumference
The length of a circle's edge – the distance all the way around it

Diameter
A straight line that passes from one side of a circle to the other through its centre

Area
The total space inside a circle's circumference

Chord
A straight line that links two points on the circumference, without passing through the centre

Arc
A section of a circle's circumference

Centre

Sector
A wedge of a circle, with three sides: two radii and an arc

Radius
A straight line from the centre of a circle to a point on its circumference

Tangent
A straight line that touches the circumference of a circle at just one point

WHICH PART?
These pictures show the different parts of a circle. Fill in the blanks under each picture to show which part is which.

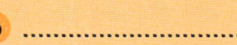

a ....
b .... 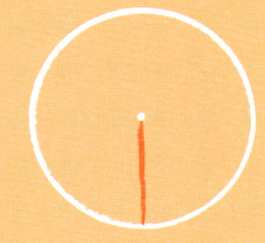
c .... 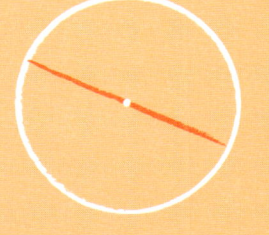
d .... 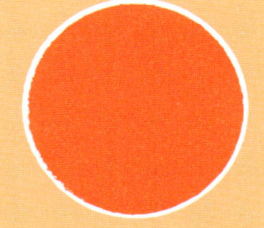
e .... 
f .... 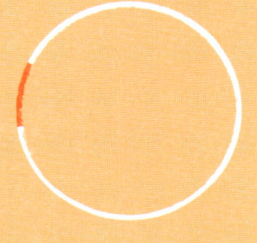
g .... 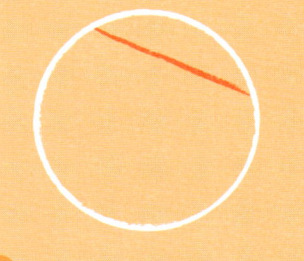
h .... 
i .... 

NAME IT!

DO YOU KNOW YOUR CIRCLES?
Can you draw each of the parts of a circle named below? Use a ruler to help you, then use a different colour to colour in each part.

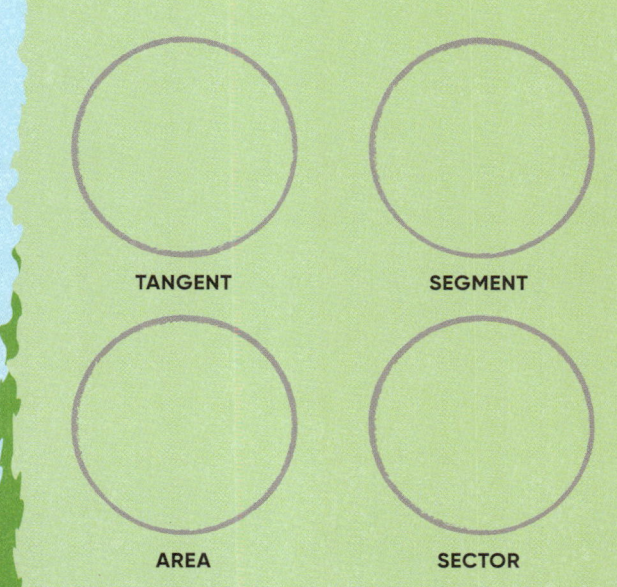

TANGENT   SEGMENT

AREA   SECTOR

DRAW IT!

UNSCRAMBLE THE CIRCLE
What is the name of the length all the way around the edge of a circle? Rearrange the letters below to spell the answer.

E C F
C   U
R   E
I   N
M   C
  E R

FILL ME IN!

_ _ _ _ _ _ _ _ _ _ _ _ _

67

3-D SHAPES

Shapes are three-dimensional (3-D) if they have three dimensions: height, width, and length. Everything that has these dimensions is 3-D, from boxes and houses to animals and plants.

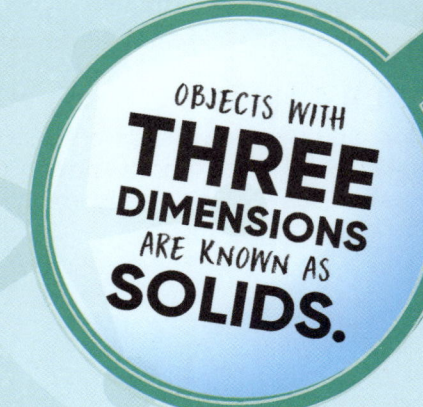

*Objects with **THREE DIMENSIONS** are known as **SOLIDS**.*

Parts of a 3-D shape

3-D shapes may have faces, edges where the faces meet, and corners called vertices. But not all 3-D shapes possess all three of these properties. For example, a cylinder has no vertices. If a 3-D shape has unequal edges and faces that are curved or different shapes, it is described as irregular.

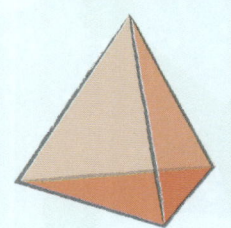

Faces
Faces are flat or curved 2-D shapes that make up part of a 3-D shape's surface. This shape has four faces.

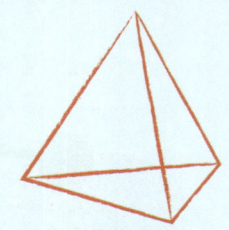

Edges
The joins where the faces of a 3-D shape meet are called edges. This shape has six edges.

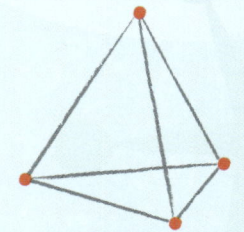

Vertices
The points where three or more edges meet are called vertices. This shape has four vertices.

SPOT THE 3-D SHAPES

Can you recognize some of the 3-D shapes below? Read each description, then draw a line from each one to the shape it describes. Not all objects have to be matched. We've done the first one for you.

MATCH IT!

Cuboid
This irregular 3-D shape has six rectangular faces, 12 edges, and eight vertices.

Pyramid
This 3-D shape has a polygon as its base. Its other triangular faces meet at a vertex.

Cone
This irregular 3-D shape has one edge and one vertex. One of its faces is a circle.

Cylinder
This 3-D shape has three faces, two of which are circles. It has two edges and no vertices.

Cube
This regular 3-D shape has six square faces, 12 equal edges, and eight vertices.

Sphere
This 3-D shape is round and has one single curved surface. It has no edges or vertices.

BUILD A CUBE

A net is a flat 2-D shape that shows what a 3-D shape would look like if it was unfolded and flattened. The pictures below show how the net of a cube can be folded to form a cube. Have a go at making your own!

1 Draw your net
The net of a cube is made up of six squares. Draw the net on a piece of paper with a ruler. Use solid lines for the outer edges and dashed lines for the inner lines.

2 Cut it out
Carefully cut out the net along the solid lines that make up its outside edges. Make sure you don't cut any of the inner dashed lines.

3 Fold it up
Finally, fold the net inwards along the dotted lines so it folds in on itself. Use tape to stick the net together along the outer edges to finish your cube.

Fold the net so the pairs of sides marked with arrows join.

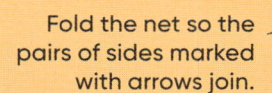

MAKE IT!

NAME THE NETS

Look at the nets below and write the names of the 3-D shapes they represent. If you need help, try drawing and cutting them out, then folding them into their 3-D shapes.

Cone
Cuboid
Square-based pyramid
Cylinder

NAME IT!

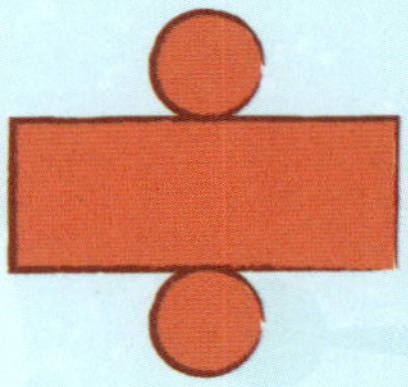

a ....

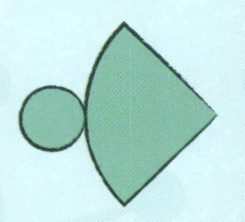

b ....

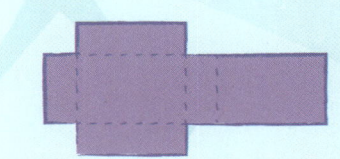

c ....

d ....

COORDINATES

Coordinates are usually pairs of letters or numbers that are used to describe or find something's position on a map or graph grid. They're very useful for when you're exploring an area you don't know or when you want to direct someone to a specific place.

Using coordinates
Coordinates refer to the letters and numbers that run along the edges of maps and graphs. The horizontal coordinate is always written first, and the vertical coordinate second.

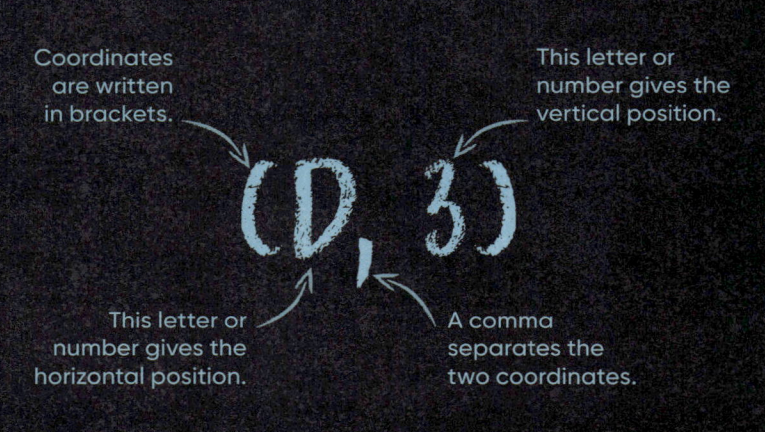

Coordinates are written in brackets.

This letter or number gives the vertical position.

(D, 3)

This letter or number gives the horizontal position.

A comma separates the two coordinates.

Move from left to right to arrive at column D.

Move two spaces down to arrive at row 3.

This square is (D, 3).

FINISH THE MAP
This map of Bullfrog Island is incomplete. Finish the map by drawing each of the features listed below using its coordinates.

- CAVE (B, 9)
- VOLCANO (F, 8)
- LIGHTHOUSE (D, 3)
- SHIP (A, 4)
- HOUSE (E, 13)
- WATERFALL (C, 5)

DRAW IT!

FIND THE TREASURE

Use the instructions to draw the path to this pirate's hidden treasure. Draw an X to mark the spot where the pirate ends up, and write the coordinates of that square in the box, right.

Start at (H, 3). Travel three squares south, two squares east, then one square south.

The treasure is at (__, __).

START HERE!

HIDE YOUR TREASURE

Why not plan a treasure hunt for your friends? Hide some treasure in your garden or park, draw a map of the area, then give your friends the coordinates for the treasure's location.

PLOT IT!

COMPLETE THE GRAPH

Coordinates can be used to plot points onto a grid called a graph. Graph coordinates are drawn where the grid lines meet, rather than in the spaces. Plot each of the coordinates below onto the graph with a dot, then join the dots with a line. We've done the first two for you.

Coordinates:

(0, 0) (2, 1) (4, 2) (6, 3) (8, 4)

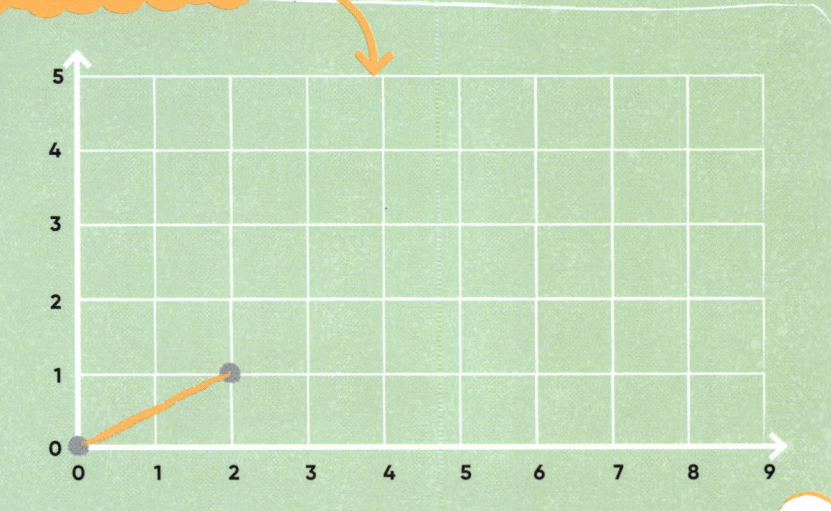

71

TRANSFORMATIONS

In maths, a change in the size or position of an object is called a transformation. Reflection, translation, and rotation are three different ways of changing the position of an object.

THE SHAPE THAT RESULTS FROM A TRANSFORMATION IS CALLED AN IMAGE.

Types of transformations
There are several different types of transformations. Showing them on squared paper helps us to see how a shape has moved.

Line of reflection

All corners of the shape are the same distance from the line of reflection.

The shape has been translated five squares up.

The triangle has been rotated 90°.

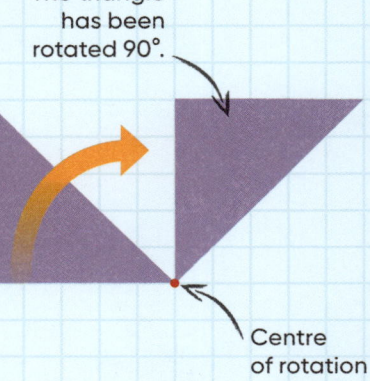

Centre of rotation

Reflection
A reflection is when a shape is flipped across an imaginary mirror line. A line of reflection can be horizontal, vertical, or diagonal.

Translation
In translation, a shape is moved into a new position, but its shape and size stay the same. Translations are also known as slides.

Rotation
A rotation is when a shape is turned around a fixed point. The centre of rotation can be inside or outside of a shape.

REFLECT THE SHAPES
Draw the reflection of each of these shapes. Each corner of each shape should be the same distance away from the line of reflection as it is on the original shape. We've done the first two for you.

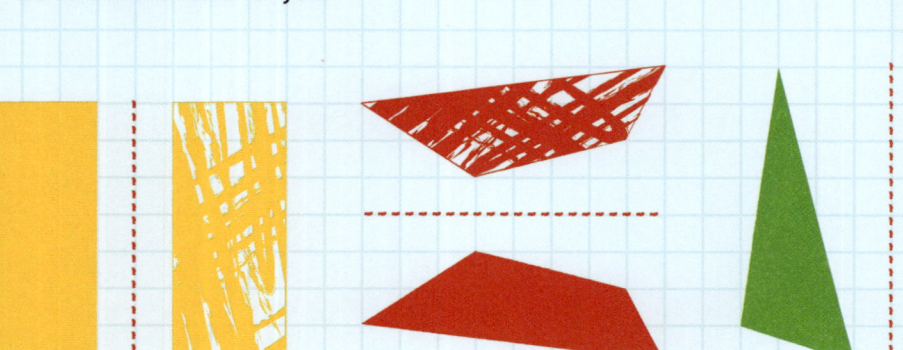

DRAW IT!

MASTER THE MAZE
Follow the translation steps below to guide the orange shape through the maze. Draw each translation of the shape as you go. We've done the first two translations for you.

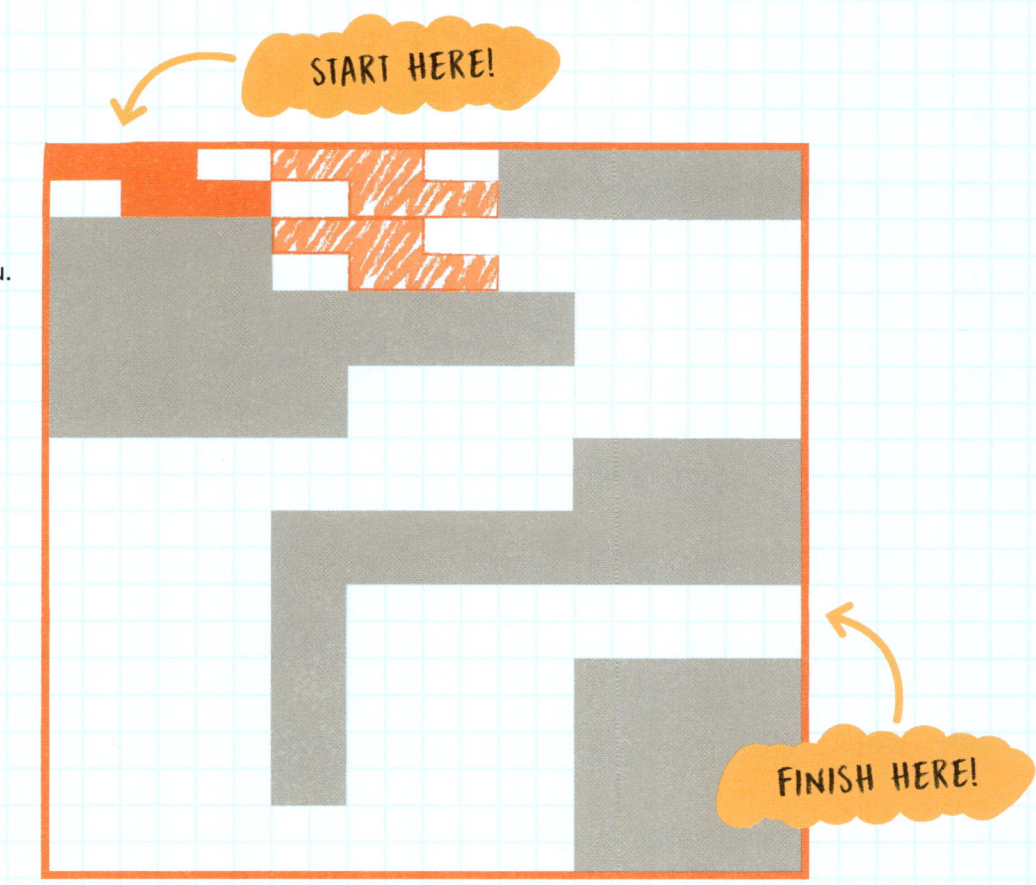

Translation steps
- ☑ **1.** Translate 6 units right
- ☑ **2.** Translate 2 units down
- ☐ **3.** Translate 8 units right
- ☐ **4.** Translate 4 units down
- ☐ **5.** Translate 6 units left
- ☐ **6.** Translate 2 units down
- ☐ **7.** Translate 8 units left
- ☐ **8.** Translate 10 units down
- ☐ **9.** Translate 8 units right
- ☐ **10.** Translate 6 units up
- ☐ **11.** Translate 6 units right

START HERE!

FINISH HERE!

NAME THE TRANSFORMATION
This shape has been transformed three times. But which is which? Write the name of the transformation that has happened for each shape in the spaces below.

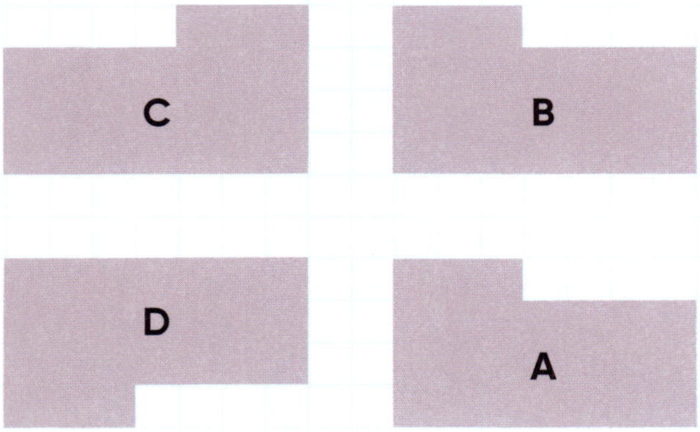

C   B

D   A

A TO B = ...

B TO C = ...

C TO D = ...

WRITE IT!

ROTATE THE TRIANGLE
This triangle has been rotated a quarter turn clockwise around the centre of rotation. Use the grid and the dashed lines to help you draw two more quarter-turn rotations of the triangle.

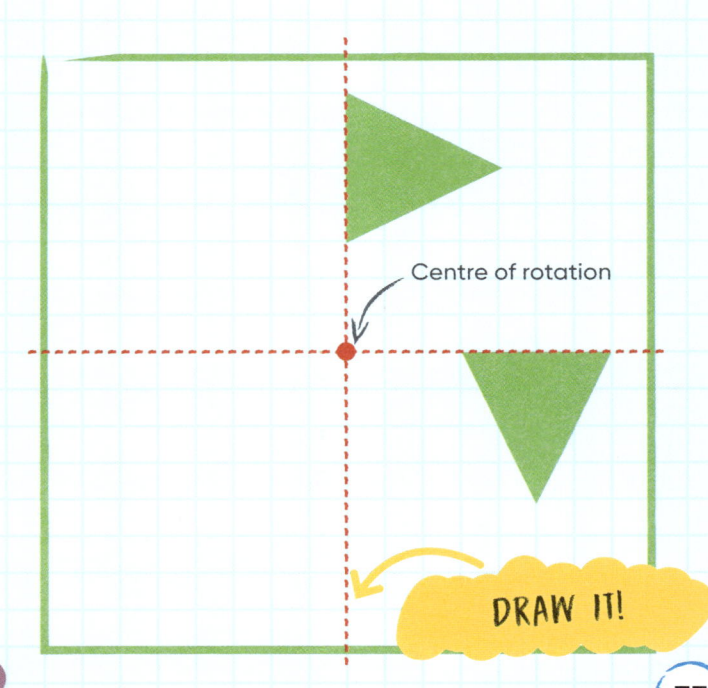

Centre of rotation

DRAW IT!

73

SYMMETRY

A shape is symmetrical if it can be split exactly in two along a straight line, or if it looks exactly the same when it has been rotated by a certain amount. Reflective symmetry and rotational symmetry are two key types of symmetry. If a shape has no symmetry, we say it is asymmetrical.

Reflective symmetry
A shape has reflective symmetry if you can draw a line across it that divides it into halves that are exact mirror copies of each other. Shapes can have more than one line of reflective symmetry.

An equilateral triangle has three lines of symmetry.

A kite shape has one line of symmetry.

A rhombus has two lines of symmetry.

FINISH THE SHAPES
Half of each of these shapes is missing! Draw in each missing half then colour them in. We've drawn in the line of symmetry to help you.

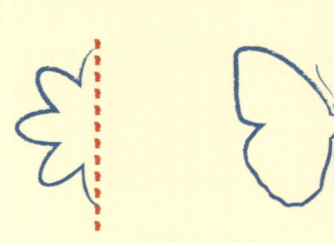

DRAW IT!

DRAW THE MIRROR LINES
Can you spot the lines of symmetry in these shapes? Use a ruler to draw the mirror lines on each one, then write how many lines of symmetry it has. We've done the first one for you.

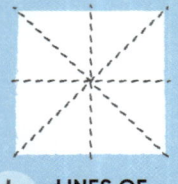

4 LINES OF SYMMETRY

..... LINES OF SYMMETRY

..... LINES OF SYMMETRY

..... LINES OF SYMMETRY

COUNT IT!

MATCH THE SYMMETRY
Draw lines to match each of these shapes to the correct description below. We've done one for you.

MATCH IT!

a   b   c   d

Five lines of reflective symmetry and rotational symmetry of order five.

Four lines of reflective symmetry and rotational symmetry of order four.

One line of reflective symmetry and no rotational symmetry.

Asymmetrical – no reflective or rotational symmetry.

IF A SHAPE HAS NO **ROTATIONAL SYMMETRY**, IT IS SAID TO HAVE ROTATIONAL SYMMETRY **OF ORDER ONE.**

COLOUR THE ROTATION
This shape has rotational symmetry of order four. Two of its rotations are shown here. Colour in the last shape to show its other possible rotation.

COLOUR IT!

Rotational symmetry
A shape has rotational symmetry when it can be rotated around a point and still fit exactly into its original outline. The number of times it can turn and fit into its outline is called its order of rotational symmetry.

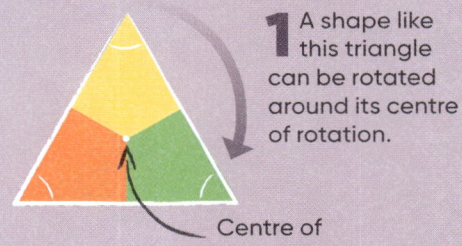

1 A shape like this triangle can be rotated around its centre of rotation.

Centre of rotation

2 When rotated a small amount, this triangle still fits into its outline.

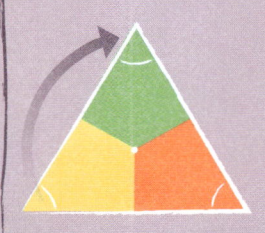

3 When rotated more, it fits the outline once more. We can say it has rotational symmetry of order three.

COLLECTING DATA

The word "data" means information, and a group of data points is called a data set. In maths, we can collect data using surveys, then organize it using graphs, charts, and tables. This can help us to better understand large amounts of information.

Tally marks and frequency
Tally marks are little lines you draw to quickly keep count of things. To use them, you simply draw a small, straight line to count each item or object. Once you've finished, you can count up the marks and write the total as a number. This number is called the frequency.

The first four marks are written beside each other.

The fifth mark is drawn through the first four.

| | | ||| |||| |||| |||| | |||| ||
1 2 3   4   5   6   7

There are seven marks, so the frequency is 7.

Surveys
You can use a survey to gather data. In a survey, we ask questions to an individual or group and record the answers. For example, you could find out what is the most popular insect in your class by asking each person "What's your favourite insect?". Looking at the totals can give us a good picture of the preferences of the group.

WHAT'S YOUR FAVOURITE INSECT?
- BUTTERFLY ☐
- BEE ☐
- LADYBIRD ☐
- ANT ☒
- CRICKET ☐

TALLY IT UP
Can you spot all the different animals scattered across these two pages? Use tally marks to record how many of each animal you can see in the spaces provided.

How many more ants are there than ladybirds? ......

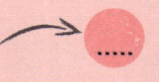

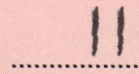

|||

COUNT THE BUTTERFLIES

A frequency table summarizes how many times things occur in a data set. The data is recorded as tally marks, and then the frequency is recorded as a number. Complete this table by counting the different butterflies in the picture below. We've done the first one for you. Circle the butterfly colour that has the highest frequency.

WHAT IS THE MOST COMMON COLOUR OF BUTTERFLY?

COLOUR	TALLY	FREQUENCY
White	||	2
Red		
Orange		
Blue		
Purple		

COUNT IT!

BE AN INVESTIGATOR

Now come up with your own survey! You could count the animals in your garden or local park, or ask your friends what their favourite food is. Once you've gathered the answers, record your data in a table with one column for tally marks and another column for frequency.

TALLY IT!

GRAPHS AND CHARTS

REAL LIFE
People use graphs and charts for all sorts of things, from analysing weather patterns and house prices to tracking earthquake tremors or a person's heartbeat.

When you collect data (a set of information such as numbers) it can be helpful to organize it and present the information in graphs or charts. This can make the information easier to read and understand.

PLOT THE LINE GRAPH

Use the data in the table below to help you plot the points on the line graph, then join the points to reveal how the temperature changed across the week. What was the difference in temperature between the warmest and coolest days? We've plotted the first two for you.

PLOT IT!

DATA

DAY	TEMPERATURE (°C)
MONDAY	3
TUESDAY	6
WEDNESDAY	12
THURSDAY	13
FRIDAY	11
SATURDAY	7
SUNDAY	4

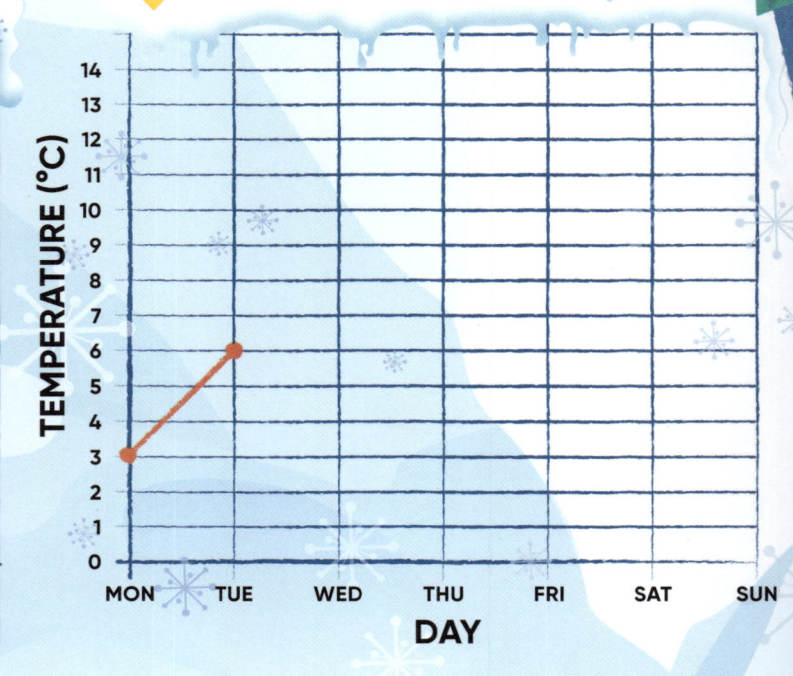

Types of graphs and charts

There are lots of different types of graphs and charts, from ones that use coloured blocks to represent data to others that use dots and lines. The best one to use depends on the sort of data you have.

The line shows how the data changed over time – rainfall increased between July and August.

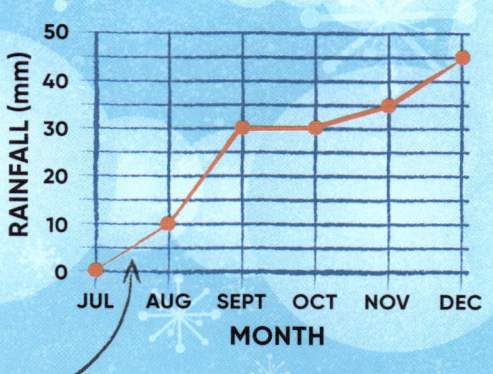

Line graph
Line graphs are useful for data that has been collected over time. Each piece of information is marked with a dot, then lines are drawn to join the dots together.

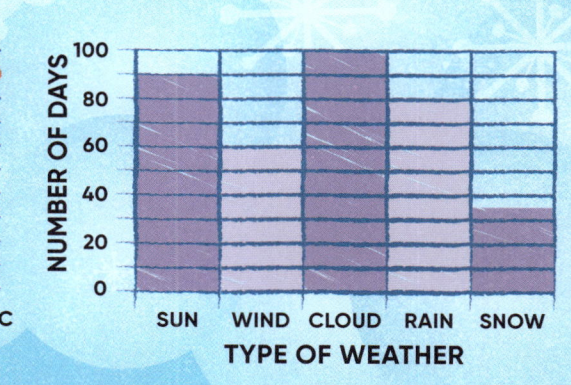

Bar chart
Bar charts use blocks to represent groups of data. The bars can be horizontal or vertical, and their height or length represents the size of each group of data.

DATA

MONTH	JAN	FEB	MAR	APR	MAY	JUN	JUL	AUG	SEP	OCT	NOV	DEC
HOURS OF DAYLIGHT	7	9	12	15	17	19	18	16	13	10	8	6

COMPLETE THE BAR CHART

This bar chart shows how the number of hours of daylight changes across the year in Norway. Use the data in the table above to finish it off. The top of each bar should line up with the correct number of hours on the left. We've done the first one for you.

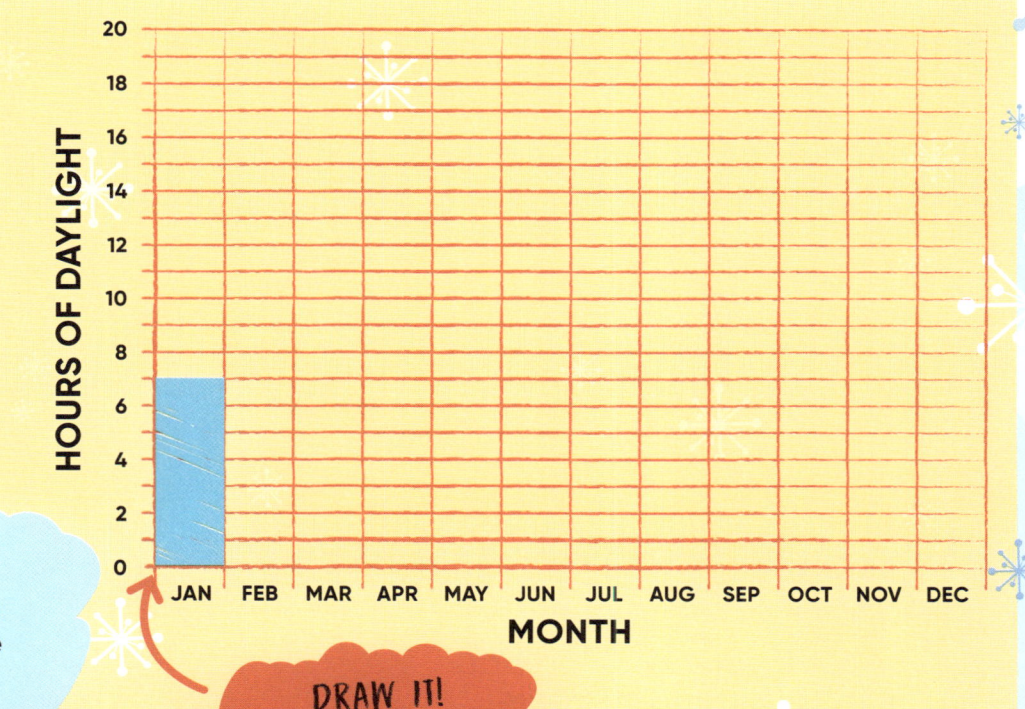

DRAW IT!

BONUS ACTIVITY
Look up the average rainfall for the past 12 months where you live, then have a go at making your own line graph.

MATHS QUIZ

So, how much attention have you been paying while you've been reading? Answer the questions below to test yourself! You can take a peek back at earlier pages for help if you need to. Good luck!

HOW DID YOU DO?
Once you have answered the questions, you can check your answers at the back of the book. How many did you get right?

19–27 You're a maths wizard!

10–18 Not too far from the top spot!

0–9 Have another read then try again.

1 What is this symbol used to represent?

∞

☐ Multiply
☐ Decimal point
☐ Infinity
☐ Right angle

2 How much is left of each of these pies? Give the answers as fractions.

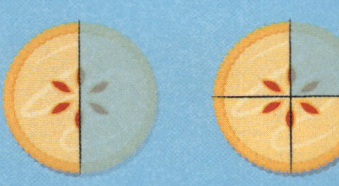

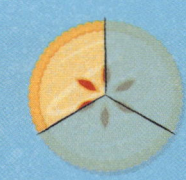

a .... b .... c .... d ....

3 The number 523 has 5 hundreds, 3 tens, and 2 ones.

☐ True   ☐ False

4 Fill in the next term in each of these sequences:

a 2, 5, 8, 11, ...
b 5, 10, 20, 40, ...
c 3, 10, 24, 52, ...
d 80, 40, 20, 10, ...

5 4 + 4 + 4 is the same as 4 × 3.

☐ True ☐ False

6 What is the name of a regular polygon with 8 equal sides?

....

7 How many flying planes, including this one, have you spotted in this book?

....

8 Volume is the amount of space inside the outline of a 2-D shape.

☐ True ☐ False

9 An obtuse angle measures between 90° and 180°.

☐ True ☐ False

10 What is the name for two lines that meet at right angles (90°) to each other?

☐ Diagonal
☐ Vertical
☐ Parallel
☐ Perpendicular

11 If Yenmai leaves for school at 8 am and her journey takes an hour and a half, what time will she arrive at school?

....

12 What numbers are missing from these subtraction calculations?

a 26 − 11 = ...
b 16 − ...... = 4
c ...... − 32 = 62
d 52 − 17 = ...

13 Which of these nets will **not** form a cube?

a   b

c   d

14 Name these types of triangle.

a ....
....

b ....
....

c ....
....

d ....
....

15 Which of these symbols means "divide"?

a +   b ÷   c ×   d −

81

MATHS IN NATURE

The natural world is full of maths. Geometrical shapes are everywhere, and often appear in repeating patterns. Many plants and animals are even symmetrical! Colour in this picture, then draw some of the things you see in the panel on the right.

COLOUR IT!

WHAT DO YOU SEE?
Find the five things listed below and draw them in the boxes.

A pattern of repeating hexagons

A shape with reflective symmetry

A shape with rotational symmetry

Circles

A spiral

DRAW IT!

83

GLOSSARY

Acute angle
An angle less than 90 degrees.

Adjacent
Next to each other, for example the sides or angles in a shape.

Angle
A measure of the amount of turn between two lines meeting at a point. Angles are measured in units called degrees.

Apex
The topmost point of any shape.

Arc
A curved line that forms part of the circumference of a circle.

Area
The amount of space inside any closed 2-D shape.

Asymmetrical
An asymmetrical shape has no reflective or rotational symmetry.

Addition
Working out the sum of a group of numbers. Addition is represented by the symbol +.

Bar chart
A diagram that shows data as bars of different heights.

Chord
A straight line that joins two points on a circle's circumference without going through its centre.

Circumference
The distance around the edge of a circle.

Coordinates
Pairs of numbers or letters that describe the position of a point on a grid or something on a map.

Data
Information that has been collected and can be compared.

Decimal
Relating to the number 10 (and to tenths, hundredths, and so on). A decimal number is written using a decimal point.

Decimal point
A dot that separates whole numbers from parts of numbers.

Denominator
The bottom number in a fraction, such as the 2 in ½.

Diagonal
A straight line that isn't vertical or horizontal, but slanted.

Diameter
A straight line from one side of a circle to the other that passes through the centre.

Digit
A single number from 0 to 9. Digits are also used to make up larger numbers, such as 37.

Dividend
The number to be divided in a division calculation.

Divisor
The number you are dividing by in a division calculation.

Division
Splitting a number into equal parts or groups. Division is shown by the symbol ÷.

Equivalent fraction
A fraction that has the same value as another fraction, but is written in a different way.

Estimating
Finding an answer that's close to the correct answer by roughly working it out.

Face
Any flat or curved surface of a 3-D shape.

Fraction
A number that is not a whole number, for example ¼.

Frequency
How often something happens.

Horizontal
A level line that goes from side to side, rather than up and down.

Infinite
Without limit or end. Infinity is represented by the symbol ∞.

Length
A measurement of the distance between two points.

Line graph
A diagram that shows data as points joined by straight lines.

Line of symmetry
An imaginary line through a 2-D shape that divides it into two identical halves.

Measurement
An amount, length, or size, found by measuring something.

Multiple
A number that results from multiplying a number. For example, 6, 9, and 12 are all multiples of the number 3.

Multiplication
Adding a value to itself a number of times. Multiplication is represented by the symbol ×.

Negative number
A number that has a value less than zero.

Net
A flat shape that can be folded to make a 3-D shape.

Numerator
The top number in a fraction, such as the 2 in ⅔.

Obtuse angle
An angle between 90 and 180 degrees.

Parallel
Lines are parallel if they are the same distance apart along their whole lengths and never meet.

Percentage
A fraction of a number expressed as parts out of a hundred. Percentages are shown using the symbol %.

Perimeter
The distance around the edge of a closed shape.

Perpendicular
Two lines are perpendicular when they are at right angles (90°) to each other.

Place value system
Our way of writing numbers, in which the value of each digit in a number depends on its position in the number.

Polygon
A 2-D shape with three or more straight sides.

Positive numbers
A number that has a value greater than zero.

Product
The number you get when you multiply two numbers together.

Protractor
A tool for measuring and drawing angles.

Quotient
The number you get when you divide one number by another.

Radius
A straight line from the centre of a circle to a point on its circumference.

Reflection
A transformation that produces a mirror image of a shape.

Reflex angle
An angle between 180 and 360 degrees.

Remainder
The number left over when a number will not divide exactly into another number.

Right angle
An angle of 90 degrees.

Rotation
Turning around a fixed point.

Rounding
The process of changing a number to another number that is close in value, making it easier to work with.

Scale factor
The amount by which an object is made larger or smaller.

Scaling
Making something bigger or smaller while keeping its measurements in proportion.

Sector
A slice of a circle with edges made up of two radii and an arc.

Segment
A section of a circle with edges made up of a chord and an arc, or the smaller of two parts of a circle created when it is divided by a chord.

Sequence
An arrangement of numbers or shapes that follow a pattern.

Square number
The result of multiplying a number by itself.

Subtraction
Taking one number away from another, or finding the difference between two numbers, represented by the symbol –.

Sum
The total, or the result of adding two or more numbers together.

Symmetry
A shape or object is symmetrical if it looks exactly the same after a reflection or rotation.

Tally marks
Lines used to record how many things you have counted.

Tangent
A straight line that touches the circumference of a circle at a single point.

Term
A number in a sequence.

Tessellation
A pattern of shapes that covers an area without leaving gaps.

Three-dimensional (3-D)
Objects are 3-D if they have length, width, and height.

Transformation
Changing the size or position of a shape or object.

Translation
Changing a shape's position without rotating it or changing its size or shape.

Two-dimensional (2-D)
A flat shape that has length and width, but no thickness or height.

Vertex
The corner or point at which surfaces or lines meet.

Vertical
A straight line that goes up and down, rather than side to side.

Volume
The amount of space taken up by a 3-D object.

Whole number
Any positive number, including zero, that has no fractional parts. For example, 2, 18, and 164 are whole numbers.

ANSWERS

4-5 NUMBER SYMBOLS

TRANSLATE THE NUMBERS

- 8
- 3
- 7
- 4
- 4
- 9
- 5
- 1
- 9
- 10

WHAT'S INFINITY?

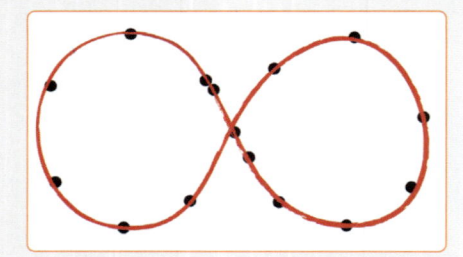

FIND THE PATHS

6-7 PLACE VALUE

PUT THE NUMBERS IN THEIR PLACES

Th	H	T	O
		3	7
5	6	1	1
	7	8	0
			4
8	0	2	0

DO THE CROSS-NUMBER PUZZLE

2	1	3		
1	0			
		4	7	8
3	6	5	1	7	6
			5	

WHOSE DOG?

8-9 COMPARING NUMBERS

WHICH SYMBOL?

- a >
- b =
- c =
- d <
- e <
- f >

MAKE IT TRUE

- a 7 = 7
- b 2 < 5
- c 3 > 1
- d 6 > 4
- e 7 < 8

FIND THE WAY
Numbers less than 154

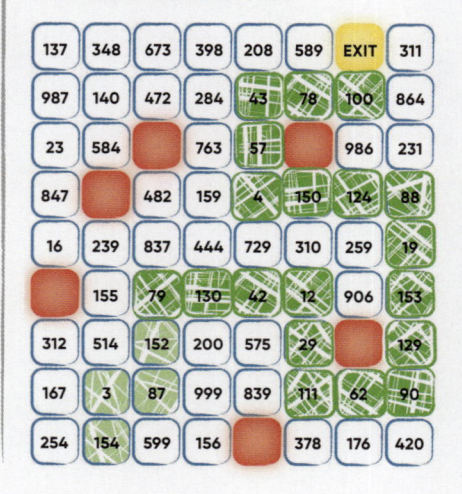

FIND THE WAY
Numbers greater than 257

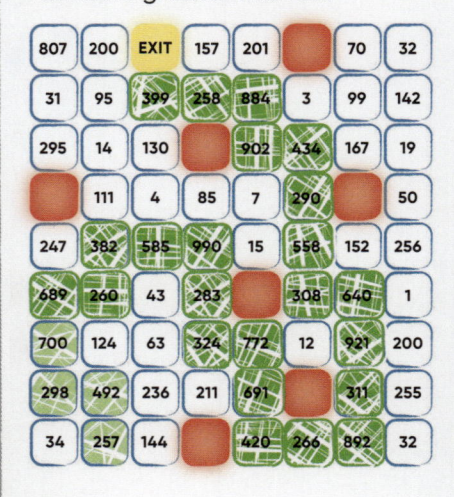

10-11 ADDITION

COUNT ALL THE BIRDS

- a 2 + 4 = 6
- b 7 + 1 + 2 = 10
- c 5 + 4 + 2 = 11

COUNT ON

- a 6
- b 8
- c 5

FILL IN THE GAPS
Here are what ours look like!

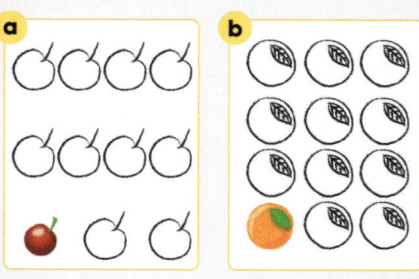

a 5 + 6 = 11

b 8 + 4 = 12

c 10 + 4 = 14

d 7 + 5 = 12

12-13 COLUMN ADDITION

FIND FLYNN
- a) 28, Johannesburg
- b) 77, New Delhi
- c) 140, Tokyo
- d) 175, Auckland
- e) 122, San Francisco
- f) 47, São Paolo

HOW MANY DAYS?
```
  1 6 6
+   4 7
-------
  2 1 3
  1 1
```

14-15 SUBTRACTION

COUNT BACK
8 − 2 = 6
5 − 3 = 2
4 − 4 = 0
9 − 5 = 4

FIND THE DIFFERENCE
- a) 4 − 1 = 3 
- b) 7 − 4 = 3 
- c) 10 − 6 = 4

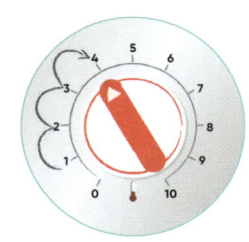

FILL IN THE GAPS
- a) 20 − 5 = 15
- b) 17 − 9 − 2 = 6
- c) 12 − 4 = 8
- d) 13 − 3 = 10
- e) 18 − 2 − 3 = 13
- f) 7 − 1 − 2 = 4

HOW MANY?
- a) 4
- b) 9
- c) 11

16-17 COLUMN SUBTRACTION

FIND THE WAY
- a) 127
- b) 315
- c) 9,615
- d) 31
- e) 289

UNMUDDLE THE SUBTRACTIONS
- a) 1,454 − 1,123 = 331
- b) 1,808 − 1,346 = 462
- c) 1,523 − 992 = 531
- d) 1,269 − 967 = 302

18-19 MULTIPLICATION

MAKE A MULTIPLICATION
- a) 4 × 3 = 12
- b) 5 × 2 = 10
- c) 2 × 4 = 8
- d) 8 × 3 = 24

WORK IT OUT
- a) 6 × 5 = 30 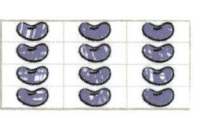
- b) 3 × 4 = 12 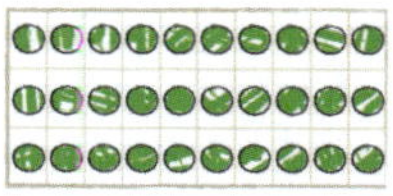
- c) 10 × 3 = 30 
- d) 2 × 4 = 8

COMPLETE THE GRIDS

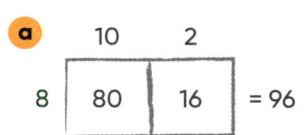

a)
	10	2
8	80	16	= 96

b)
	70	1
4	280	4	= 284

c)
	80	4
3	240	12	= 252

d)
	90	6
7	630	42	= 672

20-21 SHORT MULTIPLICATION

COLLECT THE ANSWERS
- a) 243
- b) 4,872
- c) 435
- d) 98

22-23 MULTIPLICATION TABLES

COLOUR THE MULTIPLES

ESCAPE THE CAVE
a) 60
b) 81
c) 8
d) 77
e) 54
f) 25
g) 48
h) 21
i) 20
j) 3

24-25 DIVISION

SHARE OUT THE FLOWERS
a) 3
b) 1
c) 2
d) 4

MATCH THE CALCULATIONS

3 × 5 = 15
15 ÷ 3 = 5
15 ÷ 5 = 3

2 × 7 = 14
14 ÷ 2 = 7
14 ÷ 7 = 2

4 × 6 = 24
24 ÷ 4 = 6
24 ÷ 6 = 4

UNSCRAMBLE THE WORDS
a) Dividend
b) Quotient

HOW MANY FLOWERS IN A BUNCH?
a) 6 ÷ 3 = 2
b) 3 ÷ 3 = 1
c) 9 ÷ 3 = 3
d) 12 ÷ 3 = 4

26-27 SHORT DIVISION

PREPARE THE POTION
a) 13. Toenails
b) 62. Oak bark
c) 73. Earwax
d) 123. Sweaty sock
e) 66. Mouldy apple

COLOUR-BY-REMAINDERS

BONUS QUESTION
94 ml

28-29 PARTITIONING

BONUS QUESTION
83

ADDING

a) 21 + 18 = 39

T	O		T	O		T	O
2	0	+	1	0	=	3	0

T	O		T	O		T	O
	1	+		8	=		9

T	O
3	9

b) 67 + 31 = 98

T	O		T	O		T	O
6	0	+	3	0	=	9	0

T	O		T	O		T	O
	7	+		1	=		8

T	O
9	8

c) 39 + 28 = 67

T	O		T	O		T	O
3	0	+	2	0	=	5	0

T	O		T	O		T	O
	9	+		8	=	1	7

T	O
6	7

SUBTRACTING

93 − 27 = ?
93 − 20 = 73
73 − 7 = 66

52 − 19 = ?
52 − 10 = 42
42 − 9 = 33

62 − 45 = ?
62 − 40 = 22
22 − 5 = 17

126 − 42 = ?
126 − 40 = 86
86 − 2 = 84

MULTIPLYING

a) 13 × 9 = 117
10 × 9 = 90
3 × 9 = 27
90 + 27 = 117

b) 24 × 6 = 144
20 × 6 = 120
4 × 6 = 24
120 + 24 = 144

c) 37 × 4 = 148
30 × 4 = 120
7 × 4 = 28
120 + 28 = 148

DIVIDING

125 ÷ 5 = ?
100 ÷ 5 = 20
25 ÷ 5 = 5
20 + 5 = 25
125 ÷ 5 = 25

30-31 SEQUENCES

CONTINUE THE SEQUENCES

- a) 10, 12, 14, 16
- b) 🌻 🍃 🌻 🍃 
- c) 50, 40, 30, 20
- d) ↑ → ↓ ← 
- e) ▲ ■ ▲ ■ 
- f) 16, 22, 29, 37

WHAT ARE SQUARE NUMBERS?

- a) 1 × 1 = 1
- b) 2 × 2 = 4 
- c) 3 × 3 = 9 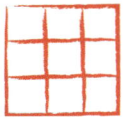
- d) 4 × 4 = 16 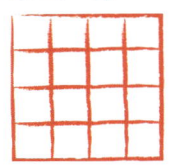
- e) 5 × 5 = 25

DRAW A FIBONACCI SPIRAL

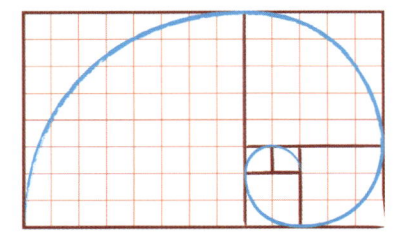

32-33 NEGATIVE NUMBERS

POSITIVE OR NEGATIVE?

- a) -5
- b) -1
- c) 2
- d) -4

ROLL UP! ROLL UP!

The circus would be left with -£30.

HOW DEEP?

It's 15 m to the bottom of the pool from the diving board.

34-35 ESTIMATING AND ROUNDING

HOW BUSY IS THE BEACH?

Approximately 72

BONUS QUESTION

There are 70 parasols at the beach.

HOW MUCH WILL IT COST?

- a) £1.00
- b) £1.00
- c) £2.00
- d) £4.00

Estimated total: £8.00

36-37 FRACTIONS

WHAT FRACTION?

- a) $\frac{1}{2}$
- b) $\frac{4}{5}$
- c) $\frac{5}{8}$
- d) $\frac{9}{10}$
- e) $\frac{3}{7}$

ADD THE TOPPINGS

COMPLETE THE PIE

- a) $\frac{6}{12}$ 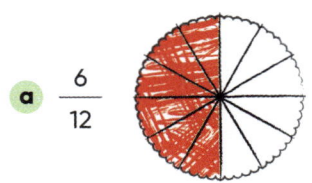
- b) $\frac{2}{12}$ 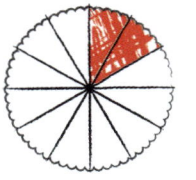
- c) $\frac{1}{12}$

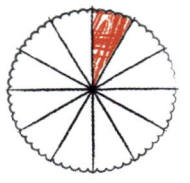

38-39 DECIMALS

WHO'S THE WINNER?
a) 10.27 m
b) 10.03 m
c) 9.90 m
d) 9.72 m
e) 9.58 m

COLOUR-BY-DECIMALS

MOVE THE DECIMAL POINT
a) 148.5
b) 7.624
c) 623.1
d) 32.91
e) 914.9
f) 5.112

FIND THE FRACTIONS
a) $\frac{1}{100}$
b) $\frac{1}{10}$
c) $\frac{1}{4}$
d) $\frac{1}{5}$
e) $\frac{1}{2}$
f) $\frac{3}{4}$

40-41 PERCENTAGES

FILL IN THE FISH

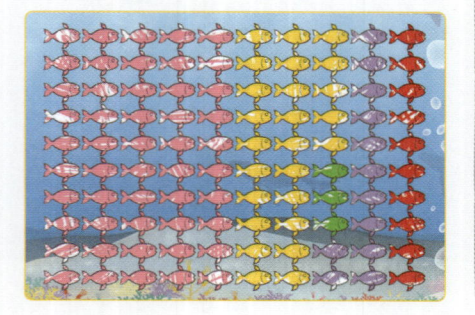

WHAT PERCENTAGE?
Parts of a lifebelt: 20%
Crabs: 80%
Divers: 50%

FIND THE TREASURE

42-43 SCALING

RESIZE THE OBJECTS
a) 20 cm
b) 700 cm
c) 300 cm

SCALE A ROOM IN YOUR HOUSE
Our scale factor is 1cm : 1m.
Here's what ours looks like!

DESIGN A ROCKET
Here's what ours looks like!

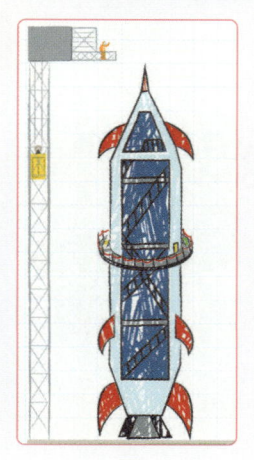

44-45 MEASURING

WHICH UNIT?
Cake width: cm
Milk volume: ml
Flour weight: kg
Water temperature: °C
Butter weight: g

HOW HEAVY?
Onion: 0.2 kg
Spices: 0.1 kg
Potato: 0.5 kg
Tomato: 0.4 kg
Meat: 1 kg
0.2 + 0.1 + 0.5 + 0.4 + 1 = 2.2 kg

46-47 PERIMETER

MATCH THE MEASUREMENTS
■ 8 cm
▲ 15 cm
◆ 10 cm
▬ 28 cm
⬢ 30 cm
⬣ 6 cm

CALCULATE THE PERIMETER
a) 40 m
b) 34 m
c) 41 m

Building C has the largest perimeter.

CHALLENGE YOURSELF
Here's what ours looks like!

48-49 AREA

COUNT THE SQUARES
- a) 4 m² (Smallest playground)
- b) 8 m²
- c) 10 m² (Largest playground)
- d) 9 m²

ESTIMATE THE AREA
- a) **Total area:** 10 + (14 ÷ 2) = 17 m²
- b) **Total area:** 7 + (20 ÷ 2) = 17 m²
- c) **Total area:** 13 + (26 ÷ 2) = 26 m²
- d) **Total area:** 18 + (24 ÷ 2) = 30 m²

WHICH RECTANGLES?

USE THE FORMULA
- a) 6 × 6 = 36 cm²
- b) 2 × 2 = 4 cm²
- c) 8 × 2 = 16 cm²
- d) 10 × 4 = 40 cm²

50-51 VOLUME

COUNT THE CUBES
- a) 8 m³
- b) 9 m³
- c) 12 m³
- d) 24 m³
- e) 21 m³

CALCULATE THE VOLUME
- a) 4 × 4 × 4 = 64 m³
- b) 2 × 4 × 5 = 40 m³
- c) 1 × 2 × 5 = 10 m³
- d) 2 × 3 × 4 = 24 m³

ORDER BY VOLUME
3, 2, 1, 4, 5

52-53 TIME

FILL IN THE TIME
- seven o'clock
- half past eleven
- quarter past one 
- quarter to four
- twenty-five past six
- ten to nine

MAKE IT DIGITAL
- a) 3:00 pm
- b) 12:40
- c) 18:10
- d) 8:45 am
- e) 16:30

HOW LONG WILL IT TAKE?
2 + 4 + 30 + 13 = 49 minutes

54-55 MONEY

MATCH THE MONEY
- a) £4.40
- b) £15.50
- c) 37p
- d) £32.70
- e) 65p

WHAT'S THE CHANGE?
- a) £20 - £18 = £2
- b) £20 - £6.50 = £13.50
- c) £20 - 50p = £19.50
- d) £20 - £14 = £6
- e) £20 - £9.50 = £10.50

GET DRESSED UP!
We spent £10.25 and this is what our outfit looks like!

56-57 LINES

WHICH LINE?

FINISH THE HOUSE

FIND THE LINES

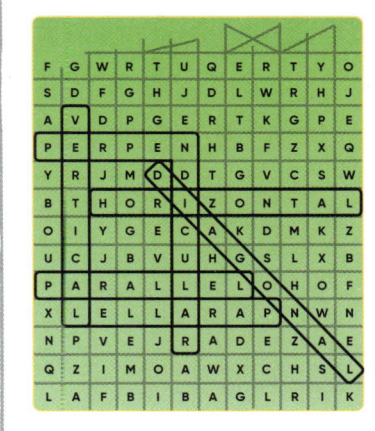

DESIGN A SKYSCRAPER
Here's what ours looks like!

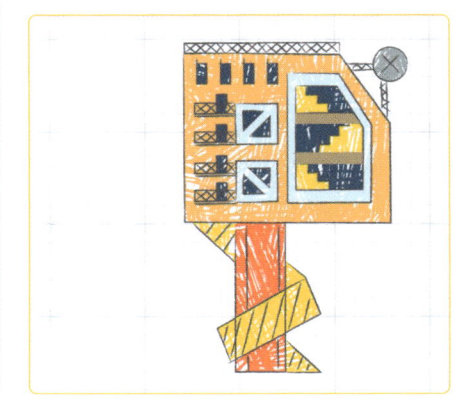

58-59 ANGLES

NAME THE ANGLES
- a Acute angle
- b Obtuse angle
- c Right angle
- d Obtuse angle
- e Acute angle
- f Half turn
- g Full turn
- h Reflex angle

FIND THE ANGLES IN YOUR NAME
Here's what ours looks like!

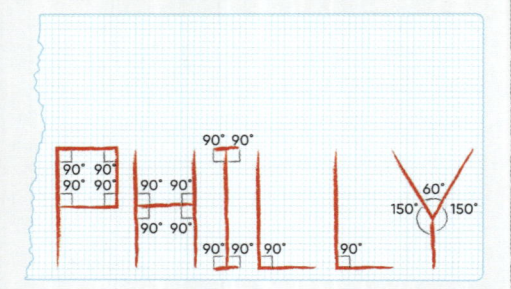

HOW BIG?
From left to right: 60°, 80°, 140°

60-61 TRIANGLES

ALL HANDS ON DECK!
Equilateral triangles: 11
Isosceles triangles: 6
Right-angled triangles: 12
Scalene triangles: 7
Total: 36

62-63 QUADRILATERALS

CREATE QUADRILATERAL ART

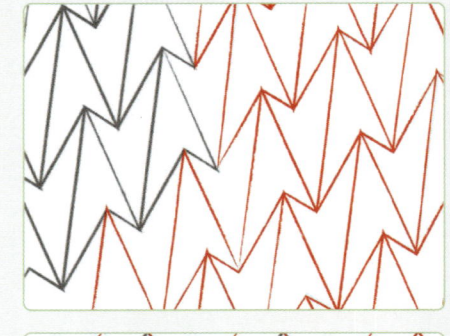

FINISH THE FLOWCHART
- a Square
- b Parallelogram
- c Kite
- d Rectangle
- e Rhombus
- f Irregular quadrilateral
- g Trapezium

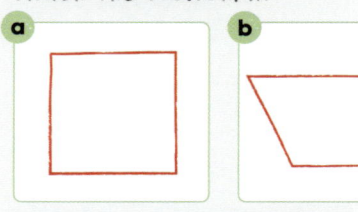

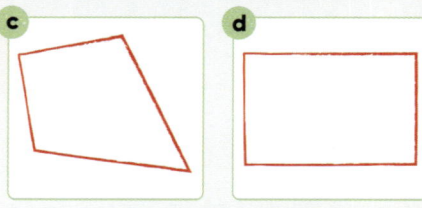

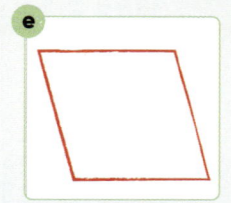

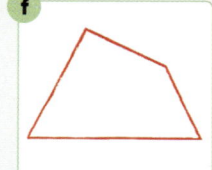

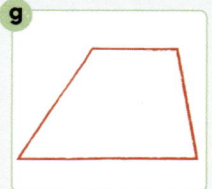

64-65 POLYGONS

SPOT THE POLYGON 
- ● Heptagon
- ● Triangle
- ● Decagon
- ● Square
- ● Nonagon
- ● Octagon
- ● Hexagon
- ● Pentagon

IRREGULAR OR NOT?
- a ☑
- b ☑
- c ☒
- d ☑
- e ☒
- f ☑
- g ☑
- h ☒

66-67 CIRCLES

WHICH PART?
- a Circumference
- b Radius
- c Diameter
- d Area
- e Sector
- f Arc
- g Chord
- h Segment
- i Tangent

DO YOU KNOW YOUR CIRCLES?

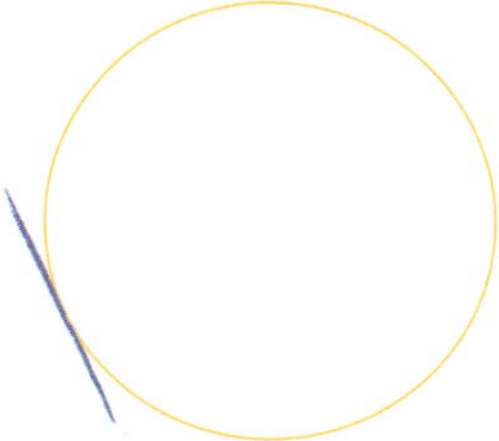

- Tangent
- Segment
- Area 
- Sector 

UNSCRAMBLE THE CIRCLE
Circumference

68-69 3-D SHAPES

SPOT THE 3-D SHAPES
- Cuboid 
- Pyramid 
- Cone 

- Cylinder
- Cube 
- Sphere 

NAME THE NETS
- a Cylinder
- b Cone
- c Cuboid
- d Square-based pyramid

70-71 COORDINATES

FINISH THE MAP

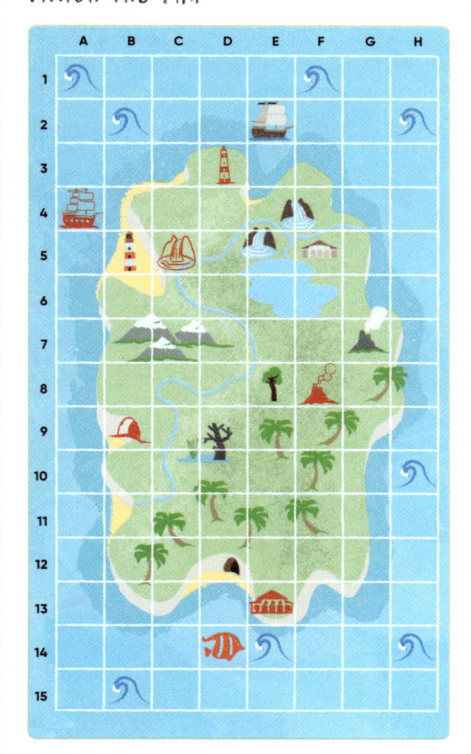

FIND THE TREASURE
The treasure is at (J, 7).

COMPLETE THE GRAPH

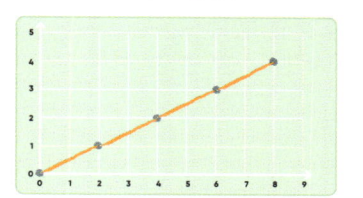

72-73 TRANSFORMATIONS

REFLECT THE SHAPES

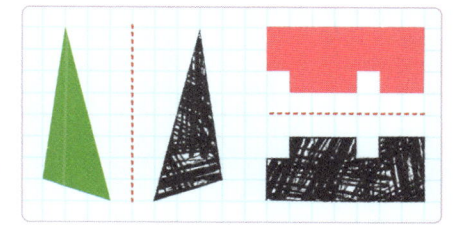

MASTER THE MAZE

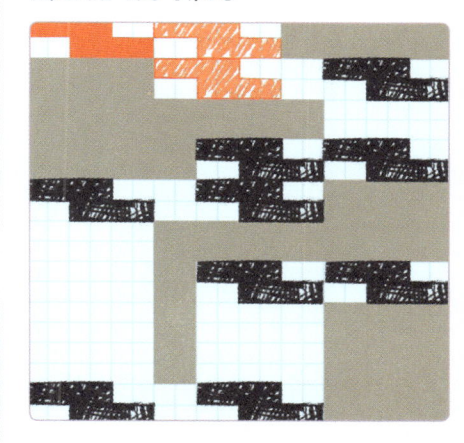

NAME THE TRANSFORMATION
A to B: Translation
B to C: Reflection
C to D: Rotation

ROTATE THE TRIANGLE

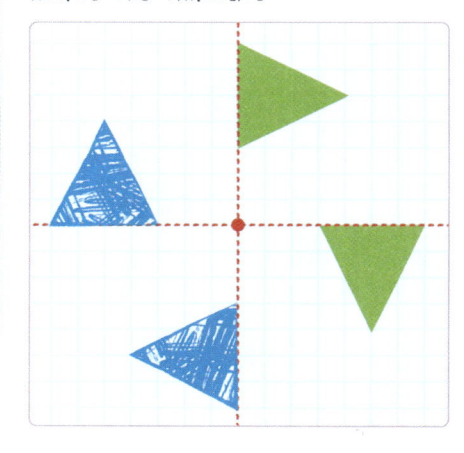

74-75 SYMMETRY

FINISH THE SHAPES

DRAW THE MIRROR LINES

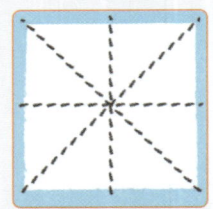

4 lines of symmetry

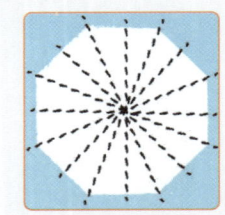

8 lines of symmetry

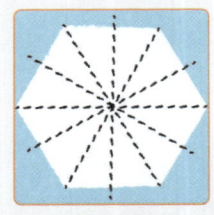

6 lines of symmetry

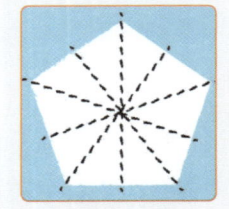

5 lines of symmetry

MATCH THE SYMMETRY

a) Four lines of reflective symmetry and rotational symmetry of order four.

b) Five lines of reflective symmetry and rotational symmetry of order five.

c) Asymmetrical – no reflective or rotational symmetry.

d) One line of reflective symmetry and no rotational symmetry.

COLOUR THE ROTATION

76-77 COLLECTING DATA

TALLY IT UP
There are 7 more ants than ladybirds.

Crickets — |||

Bees — ⅣⅣ ⅣⅣ

Butterflies — ⅣⅣ ⅣⅣ ⅣⅣ |

Ants — ⅣⅣ ⅣⅣ

Ladybirds — |||

COUNT THE BUTTERFLIES
White – Tally ||, Frequency 2
Red – Tally ||||, Frequency 4
Orange – Tally ⅣⅣ |, Frequency 6
Blue – Tally ⅣⅣ |||, Frequency 8
Purple – Tally |, Frequency 1

78-79 GRAPHS AND CHARTS

PLOT THE LINE GRAPH

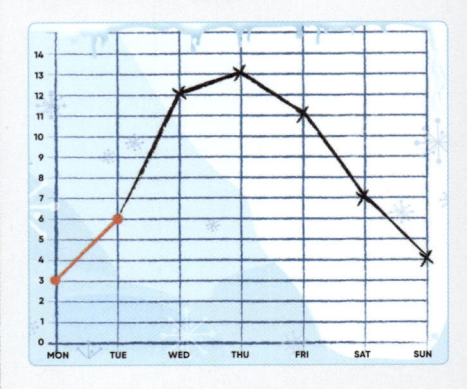

COMPLETE THE BAR CHART

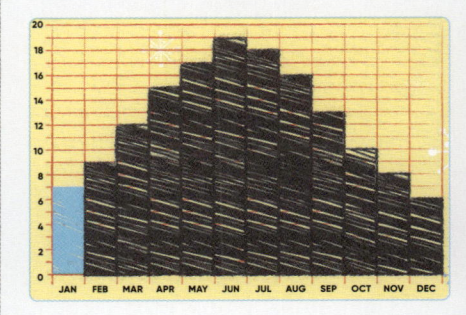

80-81 MATHS QUIZ

1. Infinity
2. a) 1/2, b) 3/4, c) 1/3, d) 5/6
3. False
4. a) 14, b) 80, c) 108, d) 5
5. True
6. Octagon
7. 12
8. False
9. False
10. Perpendicular
11. 9.30 am
12. a) 15, b) 12, c) 94, d) 35
13. b)
14. a) Equilateral triangle
    b) Isosceles triangle
    c) Right-angled triangle
    d) Scalene triangle
15. b)

82-83 MATHS IN NATURE

WHAT DO YOU SEE?

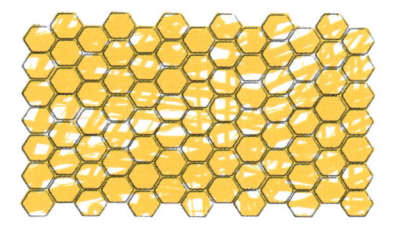

A pattern of repeating hexagons

A shape with reflective symmetry

A shape with rotational symmetry

Circles

A spiral

COLOUR YOUR OWN!
Here's what ours looks like!

INDEX

A
acute angles 58
addition 10–11, 12–13, 18, 28
angles 58–59, 60
arcs 66
area 48–49, 66
asymmetrical shapes 74, 75

B
bar charts 79

C
capacity 50
charts 76, 78–79
chords 66
circles 66–67
circumferences 66
clocks 52–53
collecting data 76–77
column addition 12–13
column subtraction 16–17
comparing numbers 8–9
cones 68
converting units 45
coordinates 70–71
counting 10, 11, 14
cubed units 50
cubes 68
cuboids 68
currency 54
cylinders 68

D
data 76–77, 78–79
decagons 64
decimals 38–39
degrees 44, 58
denominators 36
diagonal lines 57
diameters 66
dimensions 56, 64, 68
division 24–25, 26–27, 29
dodecagons 64

E
edges 46, 68
equal 8, 34
equilateral triangles 60
equivalent fractions 37
estimating 34–35, 48

F
faces 68
Fibonacci sequence 31
formulas 49, 51
fractions 36–37, 39, 40
frequency 76–77

G
graphs 70–71, 76, 78–79
greater than 8

H
hendecagons 64
heptagons 64
hexagons 64
horizontal lines 57, 70
hundredths 38

I
irregular shapes 62, 65, 68
isosceles triangles 60

K
kites 62

L
length 44, 56
less than 8
line graphs 79
lines 56–57, 58
lines of symmetry 74

M
maps 70–71
measuring 44–45
  see also units of measurement
money 33, 54–55
multiplication 18–19, 20–21, 29
multiplication tables 22–23, 26

N
negative numbers 32–33
nets 69
nonagons 64
number systems 4–5
numerators 36

O
obtuse angles 58
octagons 64
one-dimensional shapes 56

P
parallel lines 57
parallelograms 62
partitioning 28–29
patterns 30
pentagons 64
percentages 40–41
perimeters 46–47
perpendicular lines 57
place value 6–7, 16, 21, 28
polygons 64–65
positive numbers 32
prime numbers 23
proportions 42
protractors 58
pyramids 68

Q
quadrilaterals 62–63

R
radius 66
rectangles 62
reflections 72, 74
reflex angles 59
regular polygons 64
remainders 24, 26
repeated addition 18
rhombuses 62
right angles 58, 60
Roman numerals 4
rotations 72, 75
rounding 34–35
rules 30

S
scale factors 42
scalene triangles 60
scaling 42–43
sectors 66
segments 66
sequences 30–31
short division 26–27
short multiplication 20–21
solids 68
spheres 68
square numbers 31
squared units 48
squares 62, 64
subtraction 14–15, 16–17, 29
surveys 76
symmetry 74–75

T
tables 76
tally marks 76
tangents 66
temperature 44
tenths 38
three-dimensional shapes 50, 68–69
time 52–53
times tables 22–23, 26
transformations 72–73
translations 72
trapeziums 62
triangles 60–61, 64
two-dimensional shapes 46, 48, 64

U
units of measurement 44, 48, 50, 54, 58

V
vertical lines 57, 70
vertices 60, 62, 68
volume 44, 50–51

W
weight 44, 45
whole numbers 38

ACKNOWLEDGEMENTS

DK would like to thank the following for their help with this book: Catharine Robertson for proofreading; Elizabeth Wise for compiling the index.

DK would like to thank the following for their kind permission to reproduce their photographs:
(Key: a-above; b-below/bottom; c-centre; f-far; l-left; r-right; t-top)

31 Getty Images: Alice Cahill (crb)
58 Dreamstime.com: Exopixel (cra)

All other images © Dorling Kindersley